How to do
Relationships

A step-by-step guide to
nurturing your relationship
and making love last

ANJULA MUTANDA

relate

Vermilion
LONDON

1 3 5 7 9 10 8 6 4 2

Published in 2013 by Vermilion, an imprint of Ebury Publishing

Ebury Publishing is a Random House Group company

Copyright © Anjula Mutanda and Relate 2013

Anjula Mutanda and Relate have asserted their right to be
identified as the authors of this Work in accordance with the
Copyright, Designs and Patents Act 1988

The Random House Group Limited Reg. No. 954009

Addresses for companies within the Random House Group
can be found at www.randomhouse.co.uk

A CIP catalogue record for this book is available
from the British Library

The Random House Group Limited supports The Forest Stewardship
Council® (FSC®), the leading international forest-certification
organisation. Our books carrying the FSC label are printed on
FSC®-certified paper. FSC is the only forest-certification scheme
supported by the leading environmental organisations, including
Greenpeace. Our paper procurement policy can be found at
www.randomhouse.co.uk/environment

Printed and bound by CPI Group (UK) Ltd, Croydon, CR0 4YY

ISBN 9780091947996

Copies are available at special rates for bulk orders. Contact the
sales development team on 020 7840 8487 for more information.

To buy books by your favourite authors and register for offers, visit
www.randomhouse.co.uk

This book is a work of non-fiction. The names of people in the case
studies have been changed solely to protect the privacy of others.

Contents

Introduction

Relationships can sometimes feel like a game of snakes and ladders. Just when you think you've got it all figured out, something happens that forces you right back to square one.

If you asked anyone what they really want from a relationship, most people would say: a fulfilling, happy and loving relationship that lasts. However, let's be honest, achieving this can sometimes feel like an uphill struggle; whether it's trying to find 'the one', living together, deciding to start a family or handling whatever crises life throws your way.

When relationships are going well we feel good about ourselves, connected and supported, but when things are going badly we can feel dissatisfied, anxious and sometimes very lonely. Clearly, feeling loved is very important to us.

The people who give us our first experience of what love can be are our parental figures. We want them to hug us, cherish us, praise us and we want to feel that we are wanted by them. Having these messages communicated to us, or not, from very early on in our lives can make the difference between feeling confident and secure or unsure and lacking in self-worth when it comes to our own adult relationships later on. Whether we are aware of it or not, we are shaped and influenced by our experiences and our environment, and we learn about ourselves from the significant people around us.

These aspects affect how we see ourselves, who we choose to love and how we relate to others. It is through these mirrors that we develop a sense of who we are.

I believe that changing how we view ourselves can be incredibly liberating. Our values, beliefs, attachment style, family systems and cultural perspective all shape how we behave within a relationship, and these elements are what we bring to the table when we meet someone special. These are the aspects of love that we may be unaware of when we are in the early throes of romantic bliss, so getting to know them better will give you a sense of empowerment and allow you to understand how your relationship works.

HOW THIS BOOK WILL HELP YOU

The purpose of this book is to offer you the skills to more clearly understand who you are and how you behave in relationships. What aspects of your behaviour and personality help make the relationship work and what emotional obstacles may get in the way. It will also help you to understand your partner better.

How to do Relationships gives a step-by-step guide to handling the highs and lows of relationships – from the beginning of early love ('who am I in this relationship?' and 'what do I want?') through to growing older together. It examines how to successfully manage the challenges, how to treasure the good times and most importantly how to build a strong, lasting foundation to grow your relationship on, so that you can make your love last.

Love is of course a very unique and individual experience and it is not my intention to produce a 'one size fits all' approach to relationships. Relate has helped millions of people during its 75 years of operation and it's clear that every couple's story is different and each individual unique.

However, there are themes common to us all. Whether it is the early rush of falling in love, the frustrations of relationship conflicts, deciding to have children, family differences, the challenges of living together or the pain of growing apart, there are issues that affect us all – and this book offers advice on each of them.

HOW TO DO RELATIONSHIPS

I will help you unpack the many influences and experiences that have helped to shape your beliefs about who you are so far. I will focus on the influences of early experiences and the family you grew up within – and how these inform your beliefs and values, and your core beliefs about yourself. This in turn will help you to find out how much you really know about yourself, what role you undertake in a relationship and what part you play in the dynamic. I will also help you to examine how experiences with other significant people in your life also help to shape and influence you – whether they were your first love or other influential figures. This is also important to consider, because it is not uncommon for people to develop relationship-specific beliefs about themselves that are arranged around actual experiences with a specific partner.

In each chapter there will be case studies to illustrate different psychological life stages and scenarios that may echo what you and your partner are going through. I will also suggest problem-solving techniques that will help you to approach problems and challenges in a positive and constructive manner.

There will be quick quiz sections for you and your partner to do. The purpose of these exercises is, first of all, to invite you to think about your situation in a structured way and then, secondly, to take positive steps to work through problems in a more flexible, creative and solution-focused way.

You might find it helpful to do some journaling along the way, to help you monitor how your thoughts affect you. It is very easy to do:

1. Find a time when you're feeling relaxed.
2. Jot down what thoughts you've had during the day and how those thoughts made you feel.
3. Then write down how you behaved as a result.

A journal can also really help you to notice situations that stress you out and that provoke certain patterns of reactions in you. It is by understanding how you think and feel, and the behaviours that this can bring about, that you can start to take real control and make informed choices about what you want to change.

WHO YOU ARE

I will be focusing on your core beliefs about yourself. 'Core beliefs' is just a fancy term for understanding who you are, the internal picture you carry of yourself. Exploring where this comes from will be the first step in helping you to increase your self-awareness, so that you can make informed choices about yourself and your intimate relationship.

Most importantly, core beliefs are learnt. We learn who we are from a series of experiences with the significant people around us, from your parents onwards, and we then go on to internalise certain reinforced messages about ourselves. The subjective and powerful messages conveyed to us by parental or influential figures (who are shaped by their own beliefs, desires, hang-ups, hopes and disappointments) may lead us to believe that this is all we are.

However, we can learn to empower ourselves to challenge our core beliefs and learn to see ourselves more fully. Looking at yourself this way is very good news, because it means that you are not bound by your past and can take steps to transform your thinking about yourself and thereby create a healthy internal picture that works positively for you. This, in turn, will help you with your relationships.

HOW YOU ARE IN RELATIONSHIPS

Getting a clear picture of who you are will then help you to get to grips with your attachment style.

'Attachment' refers to the significant relationships that we have throughout our lives, first with our parents or primary care givers, and then with friends, partners and our own children. Studies have consistently shown that early childhood experiences can strongly influence relationships in adulthood. 'Attachment style' develops as a result of repetitive interpersonal interactions with primary care givers or parents and refers to how you relate to others when it comes to close relationships and intimacy in adulthood.

Your attachment responses can sometimes be useful and sometimes really unhelpful to you. They usually become apparent when you are in stressful situations – circumstances that trigger a reaction that takes you right back to your default setting. You may not want to repeat these emotional responses, but you may have spent so many years having these messages reinforced and over time internalising them, that your reaction to a difficult situation happens almost without thinking.

Imagine you've left several urgent messages for your partner to call you and they haven't responded. Your emotional default setting may mean that you immediately interpret this as him or her not wanting to talk to you, but in fact there might be any number of reasons for your partner not returning your call.

Attachment styles fall broadly into three categories: secure, ambivalent and avoidant. If your attachment style is secure, it means that, overall, you see yourself as lovable, worthwhile and someone who values closeness, which enables you to feel secure enough to speak your truth when things become challenging in your relationship. An ambivalent attachment style means that you may harbour feelings that you're unlovable or unwanted and so feel anxious and seek reassurance when problems occur. An avoidant attachment style may mean that you long for intimacy, but find that fear of rejection, or lack of trust, means that you avoid closeness.

The great news is that you are not bound by your past to repeat negative experiences. Becoming aware of your attachment style and its influences on your behaviour can make the difference between being stuck in a self-defeating cycle of unhappy relationships, believing that this is all you deserve yet wondering why you almost always end up with the wrong kind of person, and learning how to break negative patterns so that you are more able to actively choose someone with whom you can have a healthy and fulfilling relationship. In *How to do Relationships* I will be giving you the tools to do just that.

By learning how to increase your self-awareness, exploring your relationship journey so far and then rolling up your sleeves and doing the practical exercises, you will have the best ingredients to help you towards creating, nurturing and maintaining the positive relationship that you've always wanted. So let's begin the journey.

PART 1
Early Days

Chapter 1
Are You The One for Me?

It doesn't matter whether you are 18 or 80, falling in love with someone is exciting. It is all about getting to know that person and having an all-consuming energy to invest in them.

New couples can't and don't want to take their eyes off each other. This early stage is full of excitement, lust, hopes and bags of positive energy. This latest love of your life can do no wrong. We engage in reinforcement behaviour with our loved one. The 'me-toos' and 'I feel the same ways' are frequently stated and felt. Some people in the throes of love may send regular texts declaring their love, while others may talk non-stop about their new-found love to anyone willing to listen. Your new partner's negative sides are hidden and you work hard to hide yours.

Research shows that this 'loved-up' period can last anywhere between six months to four years. It is no surprise then that at this stage of the relationship very few couples seek to figure out whether this is the best relationship to invest their commitment and energy into.

Some people in the throes of this stage can make major life-changing decisions – like quickly moving in together, getting married or starting a family. Sometimes they come to regret these choices later.

THE SCIENCE BEHIND LOVE

So what happens to us physiologically when we meet someone we are attracted to?

Studies have found that desire and lust early on is brought about by hormones that include oestrogen and testosterone, which produce a desire for physical gratification.[1] The same studies show how falling in love brings about an increase in secretion of b-phenylethylamine or PEA – sometimes known as the 'love-chemical', which not only creates natural highs, but also helps to mask your potential love interest's flaws. Six months to four years later, this PEA level returns to normal.

The anthropologist Helen Fisher,[2] who has extensively studied the science of love, asked newly 'love struck' couples to have their brains examined. She discovered that they also have high levels of a chemical that stimulates 'desire and reward' by triggering an intense rush of pleasure. Fisher suggests 'couples often show the signs of surging dopamine: increased energy, less need for sleep or food, focused attention and exquisite delight in smallest details of this novel relationship.'

So, with the help of these two hormones and more, we are so busy engaging in mutual positive feedback that we may be left off-guard as we actively participate in one of the most seductive scripts of all.

Falling madly and deeply in love with someone *is* a highly intoxicating and heady mix of emotions. Couples often feel as though they are in their own vacuum of bliss. However, the reality is that there are multiple factors that affect, influence and impact on a couple even in the early stages of love, and if left unacknowledged they can have repercussions further down the line. Aside from the biological responses that love brings about, relationships are also affected by the context in which a couple meet, their life stage, attachment style, family and core self-beliefs.

THE CRUCIAL FIRST STEP: KNOW YOURSELF

Getting to know yourself better is the cornerstone of a happy and positive relationship with another person, and that means having a healthy level of self-awareness. Falling in love knocks our sensibilities out of the window, albeit temporarily. But by learning to increase self-awareness, you become more alert to how you feel, think and behave – and to recognise whether something feels right for you, or whether you are waving red flags all over the place and need to get out! You will be better equipped to observe in yourself what is fuelling your behaviour.

Poor self-awareness could mean feeling as though things just happen to you – 'living passively' – and that you have no sense of control. The most important and empowering relationship that you will ever have is with yourself. Without a clear picture of what you want from your life, what makes you happy, sad and excited, you are basically in the dark: at the mercy of the past and more likely to repeat patterns of relationships that leave you feeling dissatisfied and unfulfilled.

We are all influenced by a complex mix of factors – genes, social conditioning, family, friends and the environment we grew up in. How much of each is difficult to quantify, however, what it means is that we all end up with a life script. This 'life script' can influence who we choose as a life partner, what roles we play within a relationship and how we behave. Becoming aware of our personal life script and that of our partner's is the first crucial step in reflecting on our relationships and how love might work for us.

WHO AM I? DISCOVERING YOUR LIFE SCRIPT

It is important to get to grips with your own internal picture because of the power it holds over you in terms of shaping and influencing who you are. Put simply, a child who was consistently told growing up that they were a failure may grow up with this picture of themselves, and so look for those cues in others in order to reinforce this familiar understanding of themselves. Let's take a look at a case study.

———

Case Study: Jane

Jane was 24 when she hit a crisis point. She had been offered an exciting job promotion in advertising that would involve her moving away from her home town. She'd never lived away from her parents and, at 18, had chosen to go to the local college so that she could remain at home.

Jane was the youngest of two sisters. She was often described by her parents as 'special' and 'fragile'. Her older sister, by just a few years, was perceived by her parents as strong, capable and robust, and was thrust into the role of Jane's surrogate parent.

Jane developed into a young woman who often felt as though she needed protection. Her relationship history reflected this need – Jane was often attracted to men who wanted to protect her and parent her. She felt that these relationships were safe and familiar, and this gave her a sense of emotional comfort. However, she also felt a growing sense of dissatisfaction towards these types of dynamics and often felt 'caged in' or 'swallowed up'.

By examining her self-identity, she began to understand her part in her relationship choices. She realised that by fashioning herself into a helpless person, she almost always brought out the caring instinct of those around her – whether it was work colleagues, boyfriends or her friends. This self-identity also manifested itself in her physicality. She 'ate like a bird' and was often easily exhausted.

In exploring her relationship history with her parents, she discovered that her mother had had a very difficult pregnancy and had been confined to bed rest for the last four months before Jane's birth. The birth itself was very traumatic; Jane had almost died and had to be separated from her mother for several months in intensive care.

Her parents, naturally distressed by events, had gone into emotional overdrive to protect her. Jane's mother had also felt terrible guilt about being separated from her baby and this led to increased hyper-vigilance and anxiety in her behaviour around her baby. As she grew older, her parents maintained their vigilance to ensure that she came to no harm. Effectively, they had freeze-framed her as a fragile, helpless baby who needed protecting from the world.

Jane mirrored her parents anxieties in her own relationships and was trapped in a very narrow set of core beliefs about herself – 'I'm loved; I'm helpless; the world is a scary place'. The intense desire to protect their child from harm had also prevented her from positive growth.

By making the connection between her behaviour and her core beliefs about herself, Jane could begin the process of breaking the pattern of behaviour that had effectively trapped her. Understanding where her anxieties came from helped to free her from believing that the world was a scary place. She recognised that her focus for self-growth was to start taking small risks to expand her outlook and develop resilience in order to prove to herself that she could survive perfectly well as an independent young woman.

YOUR LIFE SCRIPT

This exercise will enable you to gain a clear picture of the messages you received while growing up that helped you develop the idea of who you are in the world.

Take a few minutes to answer the following questions.

➤ Am I aware of how my parents/primary care givers felt about me? How did they relate to me?

➤ Were there any labels that they gave me? For example, good, bad, star, success, failure, winner, loser, flirty, naughty, etc.?

> ➤ Who else had an impact on me while I was growing up? For example, teachers, childhood friends, friends' parents, nannies, etc.
> ➤ How did you learn about your sexual identity?
> ➤ Who most impacted and influenced your understanding of your sexual identity?
> ➤ Name two or three significant positive influencers on your life growing up.
> ➤ Name two or three significant negative people in your life growing up.
> ➤ What did you learn about yourself from these key people?

By developing a clearer understanding of who you are and what has shaped and influenced you, you will also develop deeper insights about your self-beliefs, values and self-identity. These are useful psychological building blocks to help you work out why you make the choices that you do and to work out what it is you want from your closest relationships. Having a sense of what you are looking for is important, because it helps you to understand the types of relationships that you are choosing for yourself and explore whether they nourish you and help you to flourish, or hinder you and leave you feeling stuck.

YOUR PARTNER CHOICE

Think about your current relationship. Perhaps you are about to commit to this one special person, or perhaps you are still wondering if this is the lifelong partner that you've always hoped for.

Take a moment to think about your partner selection priorities. What is essential, desirable or not important at all? (Be honest with yourself.)

WHAT DO YOU LOOK FOR IN A PARTNER?

This quick exercise will give you an insight into what your priorities are in partner selection. Rate each statement from 0 to 2 depending on how much you agree with it:

0 = not important at all, 1 = desirable, 2 = essential.

	0	1	2
1. My partner is my best friend.	☐	☐	☐
2. My partner has to share my hobbies with me.	☐	☐	☐
3. My partner must have similar values to me.	☐	☐	☐
4. My partner must want children.	☐	☐	☐
5. My partner must not want children.	☐	☐	☐
6. My partner must do all the domestic chores.	☐	☐	☐
7. My partner must be my financial support.	☐	☐	☐
8. My partner must share the finances and housework with me equally.	☐	☐	☐
9. My partner must fit in with my family.	☐	☐	☐
10. My partner must be great in bed.	☐	☐	☐
11. My partner must be good-looking.	☐	☐	☐
12. My partner must be younger than me.	☐	☐	☐
13. My partner must be older than me.	☐	☐	☐
14. My partner and I must share similar religious beliefs.	☐	☐	☐
15. My partner must have good social standing.	☐	☐	☐
16. My partner must be highly educated.	☐	☐	☐
17. My partner must be faithful.	☐	☐	☐
18. My partner and I can have an open relationship.	☐	☐	☐

This exercise will give you a clear insight into what you are looking for in your partner. Your essentials scores will inform you what is really important to you and what you don't want to compromise on. Your desirable scores will reflect the areas that you are more willing to be flexible about and your zero scores will inform you what matters least to you.

Having explored what is important to you when it comes to your partner choices, the next step is to put these choices to the test. Mark up against your ideal answers where your partner comes.

Imagine that your responses to the quiz reveal that, overall, your partner is everything you ever wanted in terms of values, beliefs, looks and sexual prowess. Well, that's great! But what you need to consider next is how you truly feel when you are with them. This is crucial when considering whether this is a relationship worth investing in for the long term.

TAKING YOUR RELATIONSHIP TO THE NEXT LEVEL

From casual dating to commitment – how do you know this relationship is right for you?

SUSSING OUT YOUR TRUE FEELINGS
Ask yourself:

1. When you are with your partner, do you usually feel happy and content?
➤ *Do you find that*: Spending time together is a positive, energised experience. Sex is enjoyable and

sharing personal history flows easily. You feel as though there is give and take, and you feel that you have similar values and beliefs.

➤ *Or:* Time with your partner makes you feel anxious, a little bit dissatisfied. You feel as though you are being talked at not talked with. There is very little sharing and you feel frustrated because you are not being listened to. Time together isn't about give and take. When your partner talks – you simply switch off.

2. When you are together as a couple, do you feel good about yourself?

➤ *Do you find that:* You get compliments from your partner, you feel enthused, your good qualities are reinforced.

➤ *Or:* You feel subtly put down. Small digs are made about you but disguised as humour. You recognise that you're putting up and shutting down. Your partner is loving in public but behind closed doors is dismissive or even neglectful.

3. When you are together, do you feel good about your partner?

➤ *Do you find that:* You are able to compliment your partner and they freely accept your positive feedback.

➤ *Or:* You notice that you are making small digs at your partner. You find your partner embarrassing in public and you resent them being with you.

4. Do you actually enjoy the time you spend with your partner?

➤ *Do you find that:* When you have time apart,

you long to be back together again. When you think about your partner, you have positive loving feelings towards them.

➤ *Or:* When you are together, you are wishing you were with someone else. When you have time together you start wishing s/he was someone else. You feel as if you are making do. You feel sad because you're remembering a happier time with an ex.

5. What do your closest friends really think about your partner?

➤ *Do you find that:* When you are alone with your closest friends, they are mostly positive about your partner. Your closest, most trusted friends are happy for you – they are able to see why you are attracted to him/her. Overall they are positive and wish to spend time with both of you as a couple.

➤ *Or:* Your closest friends are not happy about your partner choice. They tell you of their concerns and often voice genuine worry that this isn't right for you. Your friends give you specific examples of instances that they find negative. They feel that your partner is making you unhappy.

6. When you think about your partner, you can imagine a positive future together?

➤ *Do you find that:* You are able to visualise living together and building a life together. Or even having a family together.

➤ *Or:* Thinking about your partner causes a surge of anxiety. You intuitively feel that something isn't quite right, but you are choosing to bury negative thoughts.

7. Do the good times outweigh the bad, or is it the other way around?

If your responses are mainly negative and bring up real concerns for you, then it may be time to decide whether this relationship is best for your well-being.

This exercise should have helped you crystallise how you are really feeling about your relationship as it is now and bring any lingering negative feelings to the surface so that you can address them – and this book will help you do so. The next exercise looks harder still at the relationship, to see if you feel it has long-term prospects.

YOUR RELATIONSHIP FUTURE
This exercise helps you to figure out whether the relationship is something you can imagine for your future self and whether it's right for you. It might feel hard to do at first, but it's really worth it – so take a deep breath and then take a long, honest look at yourself and your situation.

1. Ask yourself:
➤ Is this what I truly want for myself?
➤ If my best friend were in my situation right now – what advice would I offer him/her?
➤ Is this helping me flourish or stifling me?

2. Then flash forward. Imagine your relationship in the short (six months from now), medium (a year from now) and long term (five years from now). Ask yourself:
➤ How do I imagine my relationship to be?

> ➤ What roles do I imagine my partner and I have undertaken within the relationship?
> ➤ How do I feel about the role that I play?
> ➤ If given the choice, would I want to stay in this situation?

If you've answered mostly positively to these questions, then that's great news. But if you still feel that there are other deeper issues at play that are getting in your way, then it is important to explore the emotional roadblocks that may be preventing you from moving forward.

IS YOUR PAST HOLDING YOU BACK?

There are a number of issues that might be at play in holding you back from a fulfilling relationship. The following case studies are here to help you explore what some of those issues may be, as well as provide a constructive way forward.

Let's look at four different couples.

Case Study: It's Just You and Me

Amy (26) and Steve (31) had been together for eight months. They had been casual friends at the bank where they both worked, but had grown closer just around the time when Amy's father died suddenly. Amy found Steve to be attentive and caring, and felt very attracted to his warmth and generous nature. Steve had harboured passionate feelings for Amy from the first time they'd met, but kept these feelings to himself.

They had recently returned from a two-week holiday that they'd been on (with two other couples), Steve had shared his desire that they move in together. Amy felt a mixture of excitement and fear.

Since their return, she'd become distant and worried that things were moving too fast. She had even started to flirt with other men.

Steve was shocked and upset. Although they'd never talked about being fully committed to one another, Steve had assumed that this was the case.

Amy

Amy described herself as having had a few serious boyfriends in the past and each relationship had lasted about a year. Since leaving home she'd lived alone and her relationships usually ended when her partner wanted to take the relationship to the next level. Her usual pattern for ending her relationships was to start openly flirting with other men in front of her boyfriend. Her emotional default setting was to self-sabotage the relationship and then explain away her behaviour by declaring that it was because her partner had lost interest in her.

She remembered her childhood as essentially a happy and secure one. She was an only child and her parents doted on her. Amy had been adopted at 18 months old and was told by her parents from a very young age that they chose her and that she was very much loved and wanted by them. Overall, she felt good about herself, but as she got older, she'd started to wonder why her biological parents hadn't wanted her. She often felt as though maybe it was because she wasn't good enough for them.

She made the decision to start searching for her real parents as soon as she was able to. Her adoptive parents knew that this day would come and were supportive of her choice. After a lot of effort, and many disappointments, Amy finally found out that her mother had died several years before and her biological father didn't wish to have any contact with her. Amy felt heartbroken. She'd hoped to find answers that would help her better understand who she really was, but instead felt even more lost and hurt. Amy had never really given herself a chance to confront the grief and anger that this had left her with.

The internal picture Amy carried of herself was of a 'not wanted' person. When it came to close relationships, she often worried that she would be rejected and that she didn't really belong to anyone. Her understanding of relationships was based on these subjective beliefs.

Steve

Steve said he had had a few long-term meaningful relationships. He saw himself as a secure, loving person, who felt that his role in relationships was to be the rock. He was often attracted to women who he felt needed him in some way. He was a willing 'rock' in times of crisis. His pattern was to get serious very quickly and move in with his partner as soon as possible to ensure that he was always around to be supportive and feel useful.

Steve described coming from a very traditional family. His parents had been together for 35 years. His dad worked as a farm manager and his mum stayed at home to look after him and his older sister. Although they weren't a particularly demonstrative family, Steve always felt secure and loved by his parents.

Steve felt strongly that his role in life was to be a support to others. He perceived himself as someone who was almost always 'okay' and reliable. He experienced himself as optimistic, happy and outgoing. This made Steve a popular and much sought-after friend. Steve's response to difficulties was usually to be upbeat and positive, but this also meant that more difficult or painful feelings were often buried.

Crunch Time

Steve and Amy cared deeply for one another. But the move from dating to a more committed relationship had thrown up some emotional challenges for them both. Deciding whether this was a relationship worth investing in was crucial.

The Way Forward
Amy

Amy addressed her fear of abandonment. Her life script had left her at the mercy of her emotions and, although she longed for closeness, she often found that getting close to someone provoked anxiety and dread in her. Making the connection between her past hurts and her current behaviour was critical for Amy, and so confronting these difficult feelings was her first challenge.

With the help of counselling over several months, Amy began to get to grips with her feelings. As part of her process, she wrote a loving unsent letter to her biological parents and another unsent letter to her adoptive parents, which helped her address the past. Amy was able to recognise the secure, loving base she'd been given – and she now chose to see this as a gift of her worth. Her letter to her biological parents expressed her sadness that they couldn't look after her and her forgiveness that they did the best that they could.

Being honest with Steve about her feelings helped her to begin to break the self-sabotaging pattern of the past. Reframing her past had helped her to move from fear of abandonment to actively choosing to create a secure, loving bond. This took work and courage on Amy's part. However, by being consciously mindful of making the effort to focus on her relationship in a meaningful and present way, rather than burying it in the repeating pattern of the past, meant that Amy was able to start on the positive path to creating the loving relationship that she wanted.

Steve

Steve learnt to see Amy as an adult and not someone who needed taking care of. This meant that he had to learn to let go of his role as her carer and start to express his own feelings.

Letting Amy know that he loved her was important, but Steve needed to be honest with her and tell her that he was hurt by her behaviour. He needed to stop ignoring unpalatable feelings within himself by simply pretending all was well, while actually being filled with anger. Instead he was able to create the space for himself and Amy to be responsible for their own emotions.

By addressing their own feelings and reframing their own approach by speaking honestly to each other, they created the template for the kind of relationship that they wanted to have. By doing this, both of *them were able to recognise that they did want to be together in a meaningful, committed and loving way.*

———

Case Study: Giving Up My Life for Yours

James (42) and Phil (25) had been dating for a year. They'd met at a friend's engagement party and Phil was instantly drawn to James. James had been a bit more reluctant to get involved with someone at this point, but found Phil's energy and confidence very seductive. For the last six months the relationship had been long distance, due to James temporarily relocating for work – this meant that they only saw each other at weekends. Having spent so much time together initially, James's relocation had caused Phil much heartache and he constantly worried that James would meet someone else.

James
James had had one serious relationship when he was in his late twenties. This had ended badly when his partner, who continued to struggle with his sexuality, suddenly left him. James had remained single since then and buried himself in his career as a lawyer. This experience had left him feeling bitter and he made a conscious decision to always stay in control – choosing instead to have lots of casual short-term flings.

James was the youngest of four siblings, he had two sisters and one brother. He was brought up in a strict, traditional atmosphere that was focused on him finding the right woman to settle down and have a family with – in that order! While growing up, James's father was often away working. He was emotionally distant with his children, very rarely showing physical affection, like hugs, and often missing key moments in their lives – birthdays, sports days and sometimes even Christmas. James felt rejected by him. He developed the belief that he was unlovable. His mother spent a lot of time with the children, but often felt depressed and lonely. Although James had a very strong bond with his mother, he avoided sharing many feelings with her to protect her from any emotional distress. He developed a strong sense of responsibility to take care of her.

Over time, he learnt to bottle up his feelings, maintain emotional distance and saw himself as someone who needed to be in control.

He knew in his teens that he was gay, but suppressed his feelings. It was only when James's parents got divorced when he was in his thirties, living independently and some distance away, that he finally came out to his family. There was very little reaction from his siblings, but James experienced distinct emotional distancing from them.

James had always known that he was gay and had wanted to embrace his sexuality fully, but at the same time had felt compelled to keep it secret from his family. This duel identity had left him feeling like the outsider in the family. On the one hand although his revelations about his sexuality had helped free him from the secrecy, he was left with residual anger towards his family.

Phil

Phil had had many casual flings while away at university. He saw himself as easy-going, attractive and fun to be around, with no trouble attracting lovers. He had a reputation for being a serial romantic and fell deeply and passionately in love – frequently. He was having difficulties with a boyfriend when he met James.

He was the youngest of three brothers and felt loved by both his parents with whom he had spent a lot of time. They ran their own family business from home, so they were often around each other. When he came out to his mother at 21, Phil remembers her being incredibly relieved. However, it came as an enormous shock to his father who was from a more working-class background and he had very set ideas about men and women. He battled with his son's revelations and, as a family, they struggled to retain their close bond. Eventually, after a tense and sometimes painful couple of years for all of them, his dad developed an uncomfortable acceptance of his son's sexuality.

Phil overall had a positive image of himself. He often felt that his charm and self-confidence would easily carry him through almost *any situation. In relationships, his tendency was to jump from one love affair to another. If he felt that things were going badly, he'd already have another lover to run to. As a result, he'd never been single for longer than a couple of weeks.*

Crunch Time

The crunch time for Phil and James came when James's contract was extended for another 18 months. Phil had found the constant separating at the end of every weekend almost impossible to cope with – often feeling powerless about the situation. Although James loved Phil, he found it difficult to fully commit and the weekday separation suited him. Although he had asked Phil to relocate and move in with him, he wasn't sure that this was the right thing to do.

James

James had been powerfully affected by his past. His avoidant attachment style meant that he very often kept people at a distance. His background had deeply affected his core beliefs about himself, which were constructed around an internal picture of an unlovable outsider. This often led him to form relationships with people who were distant or hurtful in some way. The way he chose to work in his professional life created physical distance from close friends and intimate relationships. His work effectively gave him an excuse to maintain control and never get too close to anyone at the risk of being hurt.

James's biggest emotional challenge was to let go of the anger that he carried from his past. He had felt stifled by the emotional needs of his mother and anguished by failing to please his cold distant father. His anger often came out in work situations if he felt challenged or undermined. Through anger-management classes James was able to pinpoint the source of his rage and recognise the hurt feelings behind it.

James recognised that he needed to start the process of being open about his feelings. He knew he had to take these emotional risks in order to develop emotional closeness to Phil, otherwise he'd end up repeating past behaviours.

James saw in Phil the qualities he wanted to have himself – being easy-going, self-accepting and confident. James acknowledged that he needed to learn to discover these sides of his own nature rather than rely on Phil to fulfil them for him. He learnt that in order to create a loving connection, he had to allow himself to let go of his past and create his own present. Being emotionally available in his relationship with Phil was a vital move forward. He had to start by taking small, manageable steps towards being more open with him. Telling Phil that he loved him was his first important goal.

Phil

The difficulty for Phil was that he was happy to be easily absorbed into James's life. He recognised that this was driven by his dependency issues and a real anxiety of being alone. Phil knew that he needed to take responsibility for his feelings and his actions – and be honest with himself. His relationship pattern of going from one lover to the next without ever spending time alone meant that he never really clearly worked out whether the relationship was right for him in the first place.

The Way Forward

By maintaining their relationship in its current form, James was headed for a destructive repeating pattern. James recognised that he needed to confront the anger he carried from his past and how it was triggering his current behaviour. He entered a supportive men's group to work through his past hurts.

Phil focused on his tendency towards being easily absorbed into the life of another. He saw that he had dependency issues when it came to relationships and his way forward was to make the space to find out who he was. Phil and James chose to make some changes in their relationship. They compromised and James moved back to be closer to Phil, to prove his commitment to him. They also both decided to give the relationship more time to grow and develop before deciding whether to move in together.

Case Study: Perfect on Paper

Rashpal (36) and Mitchell (33) had been set up on a blind date by mutual friends who thought that they might be perfect for one another. From that first meeting, they found that they had a lot in common. Both were very ambitious and driven. Mitchell worked in investment banking and Rashpal was head in a junior school.

Rashpal felt secure with Mitchell's strong, reliable nature. For her, he demonstrated a can-do approach to life. He loved her creative and outgoing personality, and enjoyed her positive energy. The relationship moved quickly to a passionate and intense connection. When Mitchell suggested moving in together – nine months into their romance – none of their friends were surprised. However, Rashpal turned him down.

Rashpal had been married before when she was 23, but ended the relationship several weeks after getting married. She hadn't told Mitchell about this because she'd felt so much shame about it.

Rashpal

Rashpal had had a couple of short-lived relationships before her first marriage. She was fiercely independent, incredibly ambitious and knew exactly what she wanted when it came to work. At heart, she described herself as a romantic. She loved the idea of settling down and starting a family. Her marriage at 23 had seen her take a major commitment step, only to realise weeks later that this was a huge mistake. Her decision to walk away from it had left her feeling terrible on the surface, but relieved deep down.

Rashpal had one younger sister and described growing up in a fairly traditional Indian family. Her parents had been married for 37 years and moved to the UK from the Punjab, before their children were born. They were devoted parents who'd given their children stability and a loving home. Her parents had had a traditional arranged marriage, but felt it right that their daughters could marry someone of their own choice: a love match. They didn't make any religious or cultural restrictions, however,

Rashpal's mother encouraged her to get married and settle down with the 'right kind' of man. This was code for someone with a high-status job. She often made suggestions about who would be best for Rashpal – and it wasn't unusual for Rashpal to come home of an evening to find that a son of her mother's friend had casually dropped by for dinner.

Rashpal felt stifled by this conditional freedom, but at the same time wanted to make her parents happy, believing that this was the right thing to do for the whole family. She had been incredibly brave to walk away from the marriage after only a few weeks. It was the first time she'd allowed herself to come face-to-face with her own feelings about what she really wanted and to dramatically and publicly demonstrate the internal conflict she'd often struggled with. Rashpal had taken a long time to work through her feelings and repair some of the emotional fallout with her own family.

Rashpal's rejection of Mitchell's suggestion to live together had left both of them deeply distressed. But she felt it was too soon for her and feared that she would end up making the same mistake again.

Mitchell

Mitchell was from an English background. He described his upbringing as secure, fairly happy and comfortable with supportive parents. He was the middle of three brothers, who were all high achievers. He remembers the theme of his childhood as – 'winner takes all'. This message was consistently reinforced by both of his parents and Mitchell grew up internalising this message.

He'd had a few love affairs in his life. More often than not, they ended amicably and he was proud of the fact that he stayed friends with his exes. He enjoyed the company of women and had many very close female friends.

Mitchell strongly believed that Rashpal was the woman with whom he wanted to spend the rest of his life. He could easily visualise their future together – where they would live and how many kids they would have. He knew he wanted to start a family very soon.

Crunch Time

Mitchell and Rashpal had only ever spent romantic weekends away together. For Mitchell living together was the easy and logical next step, but for Rashpal, although she loved Mitchell, living together at this time was entirely wrong.

Mitchell was completely in love with Rashpal. His menu of needs from a partner seemed to be embodied by her. He felt proud and honoured to be with her and couldn't understand why she didn't feel the same way.

For Rashpal, Mitchell was everything that would make her parents proud and on the surface he was perfect. She knew her parents would accept her choice of an interracial marriage and that this wasn't an issue for her or Mitchell. But Rashpal recognised her pattern of putting the need for approval from others over her own feelings and this time she was determined not to get swept up by someone else's needs.

The Way Forward

Rashpal and Mitchell realised that they really needed to take the pressure off their relationship and develop a real understanding of who the other person really was. Rashpal opened up about her first marriage and the huge impact that her decision had had on her and her family.

Mitchell opened up about how he'd always felt that he was in a race to the finish – and that he always had to win, because failure was not an option.

They realised that they'd both been unwittingly objectifying the other, but in very different ways. He saw her as the perfect prize to add to his collection of winnings and she saw him as the perfect parent pleaser. They had to see the other as a human being with needs, wants, weaknesses and strengths. To make their love work – they had to get real.

Together, they understood that starting by slowing down they would give their relationship the opportunity to breathe and grow.

Case Study: The Doting Couple

Antonia (40) and Pete (43) had been dating for 18 months. Antonia had been living alone after her eight-year marriage had come to an abrupt end, when her husband admitted having an affair and had walked out on her. They had one son together and Antonia was left to pick up the pieces.

Pete was 43, had never been married and had led a somewhat bohemian lifestyle. He enjoyed being single and had had a series of girlfriends – never really staying with any of them for very long.

At the point at which they'd met, Antonia's son, then aged five, had begun to thrive again, and they'd both settled down well into their local community and had made several good friends.

Pete was beginning to feel that he needed to settle down and had started to consider what it would be like to be a father.

The attraction between the two of them was instant. Antonia liked the look of this easy-going, handsome artisan (they met when he decorated her flat). He was like a breath of fresh air to her. She was normally so in control – whether having to be as the sole carer for her child or in her professional life as an architect. She felt ready to indulge in a free-wheeling, easy-going fling – it was just the boost she felt she needed.

For Pete, here was an accomplished, beautiful woman, in control of her life, able to provide for her family, who didn't need anything from him except his company. At first glance, the relationship for both of them was great. Pete adored her and felt somewhat in awe of her accomplishments and her ability to deal with difficulties with apparent ease. To him, she was the perfect woman. Antonia had a few misgivings and wondered how this laid-back man would fit into her scheduled life. She wasn't prepared to put her child through any more emotional upsets and wanted to keep him away from her son until she felt clear about the relationship. But also being in the early stages of lust, she pushed any doubts away and focused all her energies on nurturing their relationship.

Crunch Time

After six months together without a single row, little cracks began to appear. Pete would often make excuses not to show up for dates. He was either working late or was going away for the weekend with friends and had simply forgotten to inform Antonia. She had begun to feel agitated by his behaviour. Although things had started off as a fling, for her, the relationship had begun to become more serious. Her son had finally met him and bonded with him, and started calling Pete 'Daddy', which on the surface Pete encouraged, but deep down it unsettled him. Antonia had been hinting about taking their relationship to the next level and convinced herself that this is what Pete wanted too. Pete's emotions seemed to swing from enjoying the commitment to wanting to run away when he felt that Antonia was getting too demanding of his time.

He'd often intimated that he wanted her to move nearer to where he lived, but never actually said, 'let's live together'. However, Antonia had chosen to interpret his words as living together. In her mind, things were becoming serious and her child was beginning to see him as part of the family. This couple bounced in and out of miscommunications, misinterpretations and denial. Antonia, who was normally so controlled, made an uncharacteristic and impulsive decision to buy a house a few hundred yards from Pete's flat. In her mind, this would help to really secure the relationship. He became panicky and made it clear to her that, although he was excited by the move, he couldn't commit to actually moving in with her, but would stay over at weekends. This became a huge source of tension. Antonia felt very let down. She'd spent thousands of pounds moving house and invested time in nurturing her perfect family ideal.

Antonia

Antonia was the eldest of three children. She described herself as a 'good girl'. She supported her younger siblings with homework, helped in the home and was the perfect daughter. Her father was a very strict and controlling man, and wanted her to become a surgeon. She wanted to become a singer. Every time she talked to her mum about her frustrations to pursue the career she wanted, her mum would cry and create a real emotional drama. She would complain of headaches every time Antonia mentioned her passion for singing. This became a dreadful psychological game between her parents and herself. Antonia's father would feel let down by his daughter's desires and become moody and distant, and her mother would cry. Subsequently, Antonia learnt to suppress her voice and became a people pleaser, and appeared to do as she was told.

This pattern played out in her other relationships too. Antonia had mastered a way of creating a situation that she wanted, in a very indirect manner, by initially pleasing the person she was with by being the perfect wife, girlfriend or best friend, and then expecting to get what she wanted as a result. She would often become ill if she felt her needs weren't being met and would take on the victim stance if the answer was no. She never seemed to get angry, but would become distant and silent when she felt frustrated.

This passive-aggressive style, which she was now exhibiting with Pete, made him feel guilty and anxious. And, to make her feel better, he would find himself making promises to her about his commitment and then feel angry with himself for going along with it.

Pete
Pete was the youngest of four and had three older sisters. His parents had had a stormy relationship, due in part to his father's inability to take responsibility. Pete's mother worked two jobs and supported all of her children financially without any help from the dad, and Pete developed an idealised view of her. He affectionately called her 'superwoman'. He was angry with his father, who eventually left the family home when Pete was 11. He saw men as useless people who didn't commit and who let women down. This brought Pete closer to his mother and he was determined to never let her down.

Pete was his mother's favourite and, being the youngest, was spoiled by his older siblings, who protected him. As an adult, he described himself as 'Peter Pan' and always felt that life was one big playground. This played out in his relationships. He often chose *capable and strong women – so that he could admire them, dote on them and work hard to make them feel appreciated. If however, they showed signs of needing him back, he became fearful and backed away.*

This impatience to flee the relationship was now showing with Antonia. He'd seen her as powerful and he couldn't cope with her needing him. He held a strong belief that men were bad and felt that eventually he would disappoint her and let her down. He found this unbearable, as it reminded him of how let down his mother had been. So rather than deal with these feelings, he'd run away.

The Way Forward
Antonia

Antonia recognised that she couldn't change Pete, she could only change how she responded to him. She realised that she had the power to choose to be in a relationship that made her feel special, but wouldn't offer her the stability she craved. She could stay with Pete in a semi-detached way and accept all he had to offer, or she could cut her losses. Antonia worked through her feelings and realised that it was Pete's idealisation of her that she'd been attracted to. Feeling accepted in her own right was a sensation she craved. Antonia took the brave step to confront what was really going on in their relationship. She realised that she'd pushed Pete into an impossible corner where he felt stifled and pressurised to do what she wanted – just like her parents had done to her. By recognising that she was recycling her past, she saw that she was harming her present.

Pete

Pete saw that in close relationships he was trying on the one hand, to make up for what had happened to his mother, while on the other hand he was mirroring his father's script – by running away. Pete recognised that he was replaying his parents' relationship in an attempt to fix it. He focused on expressing his angry feelings towards his father and reframing his idealised sentiments about his mother. He admitted that by hiding behind his internal picture of a 'Peter-Pan' self he was dumping the responsibility of the relationship on Antonia. He had to wake up and confront what his role was in creating the situation he found himself in.

Antonia and Pete decided to end their relationship. Pete was honest with Antonia that he couldn't give her what she really wanted. He recognised that he felt happier in the early stages of a romance, but felt stifled when it came to a full commitment. He admitted that he didn't really feel settling down was right for him. Antonia realised that she had ignored her own doubts about Pete's behaviour. In her drive to create the perfect family and fit in with Pete's needs, she had overridden her own voice and compromised too many of her own needs.

Although it was difficult to walk away from the relationship, she'd learnt that it was important to pay attention to her beliefs, to acknowledge her own needs and to be clear with herself about her own relationship values.

———

Recycling feelings from your past happens in relationships; it's a by-product of living with another human being. What this means is that you may sometimes unconsciously redirect feelings from an influential person in your past – like a parental figure – to your present-day partner. You bring to the table significant others who have influenced your beliefs and you will bring a wide range of internalised emotions about yourself, relationships and the world in general. You may therefore cast your partner in certain roles, so that you can recreate your familiar script. We do this whether or not our experiences were great or dreadful. Becoming aware of this process is key to working through problems.

IDENTIFY MESSAGES FROM YOUR PAST

Working out what echoes from your past may be affecting you now can be a wonderfully empowering exercise. It is not about casting blame or feeling hard done by – it's a tool that will help you to gain insight into your long-held beliefs about yourself. This can feel like a daunting task, but it is incredibly freeing and can help you make sense of feelings that can sometimes be getting in your way.

Start by writing down what your family's expectations (whether articulated or not) were of you.

Ask yourself:

➤ Was I expected to succeed?
➤ Was I expected to fail?
➤ Was nothing expected of me?
➤ Were the expectations set by my parents unrealistic?
➤ How did my family's expectations of me affect how I saw myself when I was younger?
➤ Do these expectations still affect me today?
➤ Do I feel helped or hindered by my family's expectations?
➤ How do these expectations impact my relationship?
➤ In what way am I replaying these expectations with my partner?

By giving yourself time to do this exercise you will start to notice patterns of beliefs and behaviours that you may now be unconsciously re-enacting as an adult. By developing this level of awareness, you will then be able to start the process of dismantling unhelpful behaviours that may be blocking your path to a happy relationship.

Self-Help Tips: Handling Relationship Challenges
It is perfectly normal even in these earliest stages of a relationship to be faced with a number of challenges that can leave you wondering how to move forward. What is crucial is that you don't ignore how you may be feeling at this stage, because it is only by acknowledging and then addressing any concerns, or seeds of doubt, that you are then able to move forward.

1. By developing a very clear picture of who you are, what values you hold and what you want from a relationship, you put yourself in the strongest position to make the right relationship choices for yourself.
2. It's so easy to idealise someone and play down or ignore any negatives. But this type of thinking will in time cause you and your partner pain because you will be stopping each other from growing and changing. This kind of emotional freeze-framing puts pressure on the relationship to stay the same and can ultimately cause resentment. It is crucial to be honest with yourself and address why you may be idealising your partner. Noticing this behaviour can help you avoid this pitfall and help you to recognise whether old life scripts are causing you to behave this way.
3. Finding that special person is very exciting, and that buzz of excitement can encourage you to rush into things and take the relationship to the next level, before you've even had a chance to think things through. Slowing things down in order to build a stronger foundation works wonders in the long term. If you need more time before you take the next step, then express this to your partner. Be fair to them by being clear about how long you need, rather than vague. If you need two months to think about it, then say so.
4. Recycling the past happens without us even noticing – this comes as part of the relationship territory. Although this blurring of identities does happen, if left unexamined and unchallenged, it can ruin relationships, so it's very important to identify whether you're replaying an old life

script and casting your partner into a recognisable role so that the relationship feels familiar for you. For instance, imagine shouting at your partner when he comes home late one night and accusing him of being thoughtless and insensitive – just like your father was towards your mother. The risk with this behaviour is that continuously transferring feelings from the past on to your current partner can become self-fulfilling since how you treat your partner is likely to affect their behaviour. This may then lead you to believe that you were right about them being a rubbish partner all along! Differentiating between past and present relationships can help to stop you falling into familiar yet painful relationship roles.

5. If the thought of taking the next commitment step is causing you to feel anxious, then be honest with your partner. Being honest early on sets the tone for the relationship. By speaking your truth, you can make the difference between creating a strong foundation for the future or a weak relationship that is easily thrown off course at the slightest hint of trouble.

6. Challenge magical thinking. If there are essentials of a relationship that you want that the person you're with just doesn't have, don't imagine that they'll suddenly change into your dream partner somewhere along the way, or that you'll be able to persuade them to do things differently the longer you are together. It won't happen! Be honest with yourself, and if it's not what you want then it is far better to end the relationship than continue on a journey that you feel unhappy about.

By acknowledging what you bring to the table and noticing how these different feelings, values and beliefs may play out in your relationship, you can really make the difference between being present in the process and creating a loving and strong relationship foundation, or blindly teetering on an emotional high wire hoping for the best!

Chapter 2
Meet the Family

Once we feel positive and secure about a new relationship, introducing them to our family is very often the next step. For most of us, it matters that our family likes our partner. Why? Because these people form an integral part of our psychological well-being: support, sharing and caring.

For some, family means the family they grew up in, and for others this means friends who have become like family – chosen family. Most people would probably agree that they want nothing more than for the people they feel closest to and their partner to develop a strong and positive connection, and that they hope that introducing their partner to their family turns out to be a joyous occasion. But the reality is that it can feel like an incredibly daunting task and sometimes it goes very badly wrong. Why should doing something so positive carry so many problems?

Families, by their very nature, have their own scripts which consist of boundaries, rules, traditions, behaviours, prejudices, roles that they play in your life and certain beliefs that may have been passed down for generations. Your family may have a closed-off attachment style and therefore feel unhappy to throw their doors open to new people, or your family may be very laissez-faire and have loose boundaries, for instance where they don't mind walking around in their underwear at weekends – something which could potentially scare your partner away!

Your family members will also have their own way in which they see you and treat you, as well as core beliefs that they hold about you and expectations that they have of you. They may have freeze-framed you somewhere in the past and therefore continue to see you as a small, boisterous child who needs protecting, or the sulky teenager who remains the avoidant outsider. When you are with your family, you may also revert back to child-like behaviour, where you all slot into familiar patterns of behaviour from the past.

Whether you are very close to your family or only politely shake hands on special occasions, introducing a new partner brings about an emotional shift for them as well as intense feelings for you.

There is no doubt that your family will experience their own cycle of emotions. Even the most loving families will have powerful reactions to a new person coming into the family and into their world. This is the context you are taking your partner into. Preparing both your partner and your family is vital, and it needs your proper attention. Dropping your partner into a room full of your relations and then fleeing the scene hoping for the best isn't going to work.

In this chapter, I am going to focus on a step-by-step approach and explore what can really help you, your partner and your family to have a positive encounter and develop a solid foundation.

INTRODUCING YOUR PARTNER

It is important to discuss with your partner if either family is likely to have any issues with your partner choice. If the answer is yes, then you need to think about what the best way forward is, and I give advice on this later in this chapter. It is vital to be clear about what both partners' needs are and to be able to give and take with one another.

BEFORE INTRODUCING YOUR PARTNER TO YOUR FAMILY
Ask yourself:

➤ How will introducing my partner to my family affect them?
➤ What would help/hinder the encounter?
➤ What am I hoping for from their first encounter?
➤ What is my fantasy about the first meeting?
➤ What is my nightmare about the first meeting?
➤ What do I really want to happen from their first meeting and afterwards?

These questions will help you to have realistic goals and expectations, and clarify in your own mind if both parties meeting is something that you want to happen. There may be very good reasons not to make introductions at all; for instance, in circumstances where relationships with family are already very negative, unstable or even toxic, and introductions would adversely affect an otherwise positive relationship with your partner.

Self-Help Tips: Introducing the Family

1. Step by step is by far the wisest strategy.
2. Make sure your parents are really ready to meet your partner.
3. Minimise the stress around it and ensure that the first meeting is a low-key affair. So instead of Christmas weekend with the whole family, how about a small, relaxed, informal meal with the parents?

4. Give your partner the heads-up on your family's dynamics and style of communicating. Whether they are all hugs and laughter or physically distant and don't talk much, let your partner know.
5. Let your family know too what your partner is comfortable and uncomfortable with.
6. Don't leave all the politeness and effort to your partner, put your best self forward – this will communicate to your family that you care about what they think and respect their boundaries. Hopefully, this will set the tone for the next meeting, but be prepared for things to take time and be prepared to exercise patience with them.

THE CHALLENGES

Every family has their hot-button issues, particular ways of operating and styles of communicating. Your partner will also have their own life script that they will be bringing into the encounter too. So understanding where both parties are coming from and preparing them in a constructive way is the key to success in most cases.

There are common areas that some families may find difficult and challenging. Broadly speaking, these encompass: sexuality; coming from different backgrounds, whether that is race, religion or class; if you and your partner are at different life stages – much older or much younger; and if your partner has been married before or has children from a previous relationship.

There are some fears and prejudices that can emerge only when families are challenged to embrace your choice of partner. When it comes to the issue of race, you may discover that these feelings are very deep-seated, which can mean that your family may never approve of your partner.

You may have a situation where some members of your family are fine with your partner but others are not. You could get accused of splitting up the family because of your choices.

Your partner may be very open, but their parents may not be. You may be very accepting, but your parents may be horrified by your choices. Understanding how to work positively within the framework of your family system is key to helping your relationship thrive.

RACIAL DIFFERENCES

The subject of race is an emotional one. When you introduce a partner of a different race to a family, expected or unexpected prejudices can be thrown up from certain family members. These attitudes may have for the most part gone unchallenged in the past because they weren't so close to home. Your family may have been okay with you having friends from a different racial background to yours, but react very differently when it comes to your partner being racially different.

You could find there will be a number of defensive barriers that families or particular family members put up that can cause tension for years. Their prejudices may stem from long-held beliefs about different cultures and ethnic groups, and it may be that stereotypes that are perpetuated in the media or elsewhere have continued to validate these beliefs. They may have a genuine fear that you will come to harm unless you find someone from a similar background, with whom they can connect to. This fear can stem from lack of contact with people from different backgrounds in their own social group. Your family may worry about how to behave around someone whom they perceive as very different from themselves. They could believe that they have to be careful what they say in order not to cause offence.

For some it may be about coming from a different caste, ethnic group or choosing not to have an arranged marriage that causes family tensions.

There are many factors that can lie beneath all of this: fear of change, the security of long-held beliefs, resistance to more flexible thinking, fear of losing you to something that appears threatening to them or a deeply ingrained belief that has been passed down over generations. Whatever the root of their reactions, it can make the thought of introducing your partner very challenging.

———

Case Study: More Similar than Different

Laura (25) was of Irish descent but brought up in the West Country and Ravinder (25) was of Indian heritage but born and brought up in Essex. They had been together for five years. They met while studying Law at the same university. They'd become extremely close very quickly and moved in together in their final year. When they finished their studies, they spent six months travelling around Europe and, on their return, they found a flat to rent together. Laura was very serious about Ravinder and he had met her family several times. They really liked him and were very happy that the two of them had settled down together. Ravinder on the other hand hadn't told his family about Laura. Although his parents described themselves as very open-minded, they did want their son to marry someone from an Indian background.

Ravinder, as the oldest son with one younger brother, was acutely aware of this. The longer his relationship went on with Laura, the harder he found it to tell them. He had been open with Laura about what he was going through. He felt that his family would really struggle to accept her and didn't quite know how to make it work. But she had begun to feel as though he was ashamed of her and that he was far more committed to his family than he was to her. This was beginning to take its toll on their relationship, and, feeling desperately upset, Laura had threatened to ring his mother up and introduce herself.

Ravinder

Ravinder's family had lived in Britain since the 1950s. His grandparents lived only a few miles away and the family were well established in the local community, where his father owned a catering business. Ravinder had been encouraged to study law and get a good career, so that he could have financial security and be in a 'proper' job. As the oldest, Ravinder had always been expected to do the right thing. He was the 'golden boy' – high achieving and respectful. His younger brother had dropped out of school at 16, dated a string of girls, smoked and drank, and seemed to get away with being the rebel. There was just an 18-month age gap between the two boys, but they were so different and weren't particularly close. Ravinder felt as though he was always the one bailing out his younger brother, who in turn felt that he was ignored by their parents, because he wasn't special. All hopes for family honour lay with Ravinder. He didn't want to let his family down, but he also loved Laura deeply. He felt inner turmoil, because he experienced Laura's family as warm and accepting people, who he really believed his parents would get along with if they just let themselves be open.

Ravinder felt as if he was living two separate lives, which he hated, and he often felt like a fraud when he went to visit his parents and lied about not having met anyone special.

Laura

Laura's family were originally from Dublin. Her parents had split up when she was nine, and Laura and her mother had moved away when Laura's mother remarried. Laura had one stepsister. Laura's father also remarried and had two sons.

Laura maintained a close relationship with her father, whom she saw fairly regularly. There was an agreement that Laura's parents had made when they split up that he would be included in important events in Laura's life. He was there when she graduated and Laura was very keen to get his approval when she introduced Ravinder to him.

Because Laura had a different blueprint of family life, she couldn't comprehend why Ravinder was so closed down when it came to his family and she confided her disappointment to her mother about not meeting Ravinder's parents. Family was very important to her and she felt that this exclusion was a bad sign. Laura's mother had offered to invite his family over to their family home but Ravinder had rejected this plan out of hand, fearing it would be disastrous.

Crunch Time

Laura had interpreted Ravinder's reluctance as a rejection of her needs and this caused her much pain. She felt that he was just biding his time with her before he went off and married the right girl in order to make his parents proud. Ravinder felt a strong obligation to his family too, and wanted to do the right thing and please his parents. But his avoidant behaviour was causing far more problems.

The Way Forward

Struggling with his feelings, Ravinder decided to speak to his mother about Laura. He knew that this would be difficult and expected a huge emotional fallout. He told his mother that he had met someone whom she would really like, who was a trainee solicitor like himself and who was also from a different background. His mother was very shocked and upset, mainly, she said, because she felt she had been betrayed by his secrecy. She worried about what would happen if Ravinder and Laura had children – how would society treat them? She expressed anxiety about Ravinder letting go of his culture and decided that she didn't want to meet Laura. She felt strongly that they were too young to know what was good for them and consigned the relationship to being a fleeting thing.

Ravinder's father was more open to meeting Laura but worried about the fact that she came from a divorced family background.

Ravinder felt as though his parents were just putting up barriers and prejudices and accused them of being narrow-minded.

After months of tension between Ravinder and his family, they finally agreed to meet Laura for lunch. Ravinder advised Laura that his mother was, by her very nature, very emotional and that it was best not to get worked up about what she may come out with.

They agreed to meet in a neutral setting at a local restaurant. This gave all parties the opportunity to be on an equal footing and also meant that the meeting was confined to a specific amount of time.

The first meeting was tense, and, although Ravinder's parents expressed how nice Laura was, she felt their disapproval.

It took many months of meetings and compromises on all sides, before Ravinder's parents finally conceded that it was either accept Laura or lose their son.

Both Laura and Ravinder had been fearful that the relationship would end if they confronted the underlying issues. Ravinder acknowledged that allowing the situation to go on for so long had exacerbated the problems. By being in denial and hoping for the best, the issues had only got bigger. Laura realised that she had chosen to ignore the warning signs and, instead of tackling Ravinder's resistance to her meeting his family, had been confiding in her mother.

She acknowledged that the situation with Ravinder and his family had left her feeling like an outsider and touched a painful memory from her past. When both her parents had remarried and had more children, she described feeling rejected and like the unwanted outsider. These feelings of powerlessness from her childhood had prevented her from behaving like the assertive, empowered adult that she'd become, and Laura knew these were issues she had to confront too.

Self-Help Tips: Handling Negative Family Attitudes to Racial Differences

It is incredibly painful to experience family disapproval, particularly if it is because they can't accept the person whom you have fallen in love with.

1. **Speak up.** It is vital to tackle the 'elephant in the room', rather than continuously ignore your own concerns. Feeling as though you are being kept away from your partner's family needs to be discussed very early on. It may be the case that your partner will only introduce you

to their family if they want to be fully committed to you. If they're continuously putting up roadblocks then this is a red flag – and you need to speak up and confront it.

2. **Acknowledge cultural subtleties.** The family culture we come from forms an integral part of our identity and influences how we see ourselves in the world. You may have grown up in a very different culture and atmosphere to that of your parents' generation and therefore have more cultural similarities than differences with your partner; but parental influence may still have a big impact on how they relate to your relationship. This is a very important factor to acknowledge and prepare for. It may sound like an unnecessary task, but it is important for both you and your partner to acknowledge each other's culture, traditions, values and beliefs.

3. **Independence vs interdependence.** Acknowledging your family and your partner's family's cultural perspective is vital. Some cultures encourage independence as people become adult. This means living away from the family home they grew up in and becoming more individualised in how they organise their lives. In other cultures, family life is more interdependent and expectations are about becoming part of the family. This may mean living together, or living closer, and far more involvement in each other's lives.

4. **Be honest.** If you are avoiding introducing your partner to your family for fear that you will upset them or worse still lose them, then you need to weigh up what is most important to you. After all, you are going to have to live with the consequences for a very long time.

5. **Straight talk.** Be aware of your relationship being subtly undermined. If digs or indirect criticism are made of you or your partner, then be prepared to use some straight talk so that toxic conversations are nipped in the bud.

6. **Brave heart.** If your family behaves badly and switches off lines of communication, then that is their decision not

yours. They are entirely responsible for how they choose to behave. If you choose your partner over your family, then the key to nurturing your relationship in such challenging circumstances is to develop your own network of support. Making a relationship thrive takes work, and connecting with positive, like-minded friends can really help.

Be prepared to tackle these issues over and over again as they may continue to emerge in different contexts throughout your relationship – whether at family gatherings or deciding to have a child together.

AGE DIFFERENCES

Having a relationship with someone older or younger can sometimes throw up real challenges for family and friends. Our culture in the industrialised world makes two assumptions: that the age gap will be small and, in heterosexual relationships, the man will be the older of the two. Now, whether or not this agenda was set early on in our evolution so that men would provide and women would be young and healthy enough to have babies, we do appear to have got stuck with this script in our collective hardwiring! However, there is evidence all around us that reflects how the make-up of society is constantly changing and adapting – and we're making so many different choices about who our partner should be. However, this may not stop society from using an old script to judge a situation by.

If you're a woman with a younger man it can be doubly difficult thanks to society judging you. A study in 2003 by the Office of National Statistics showed that the proportion of women in England and Wales marrying younger men rose from 15 per cent to 26 per cent between 1963 and 1998. But you may not find it uncommon to hear derogatory language hurled by people in order to hide their awkward feelings –

whether it is gold-digger, cradle snatcher or cougar. Being able to deal with people's prejudices as a team will ensure that you show a united front, and nip their hostility in the bud.

PREPARE YOURSELF BEFORE INTRODUCTIONS

Before you knock on your parents' door to tell them your good news, make sure that your relationship is on solid ground. Ask yourself the following key questions to ensure that you're clear in your own mind. Ask your partner to do the same, and then share your answers. This will give you a very clear steer on what your relationship is really about, and how you see yourselves in relation to one another.

1. Is this relationship more than just a physical connection?
2. Are you with your partner just in order to feel good about yourself?
3. Do you have a solid and loving emotional connection?
4. Do you share hobbies and interests with one another?
5. Do your values and beliefs about the world differ greatly or do you hold similar views?
6. You and your partner may be at different life stages, but do you have similar life goals?
7. If your partner already has a family, will you be happy not to have one?
8. If your partner already has children, and you decide to have your own, will your partner find that difficult?
9. Are you prepared for what may change in 10 to 15 years' time in terms of physical, sexual and emotional needs?

If you find that your answers reflect a real synchrony, then that's wonderful. It is when you are both sure you have a solid connection that you can prepare to handle your family and friends. However, if you feel that you are not on the same page, and feel out of synch with your partner, then you need to be honest with yourself about your relationship.

Think seriously about whether you are over-compromising to be in a relationship that you are not entirely sure about, and what the reasons are that are keeping you in the relationship. This will help you decide whether your relationship is enough for you in the long term.

———

Case Study: Age Is Just a Number

George (50) and Agnes (29) had been together for two years. George had two daughters, aged 18 and 20, from his first marriage. He had been divorced for four years when he met Agnes. Agnes had just broken up with a long-term boyfriend who her friends and family thought she was going to marry. The relationship had fallen apart when her ex wanted to start a family, and Agnes felt that she just wasn't ready.

George and Agnes had known each other for a long time as George used to work at the same accountancy firm as Agnes's father. George and his first wife, Sally, had been good friends with Agnes's parents and used to socialise with them regularly. George and Agnes hadn't seen each other in years and were reintroduced after George's divorce at a family barbeque. Agnes's parents had invited George to the barbeque to introduce him to some single friends of theirs, as he had been feeling depressed and hadn't been socialising much.

George and Agnes got talking, and found that they had a lot in common.

George had some misgivings about being with someone much younger than himself. He didn't want to have any more children, and told Agnes this. She was adamant that children weren't a priority and she wasn't sure she even wanted to have a family.

After several months of keeping their relationship a secret from her parents, George and Agnes had decided that she would move in with him and that it was time to be open with her parents about their relationship. Agnes felt that this may be really difficult for her parents as they were a similar age to George. They decided to invite her parents round to George's home for dinner and reveal their relationship.

This went very badly. Agnes's mother was deeply upset. She was furious with her daughter and spoke of her utter disgust that George would even dream of dating their daughter whom he'd known since she was a teenager – let alone moving her into his home. Agnes's father was so angry that he stormed out.

George had told his daughters, who although adults now had also expressed concerns because of other people's judgements and criticisms. They worried that he would be seen as a dirty old man – and his oldest daughter expressed her embarrassment about telling people that her dad was dating his friends' daughter.

Agnes

Agnes was the youngest of three daughters, who both parents doted on. She was a high achiever at school, and her parents felt that she was destined for big things in her career in the fashion industry. When Agnes had started dating John, when she was 24, her friends and family were delighted and thought that they were the perfect couple. They were of a similar age, worked for the same company and John clearly loved Agnes. They had been living together for about a year and a half when John had started talking about wanting to get married and starting a family.

Agnes was excited at first, and she and her mother had started planning for the wedding. Her friends thought John was wonderful and couldn't wait for the two of them to tie the knot. But very quickly Agnes started to have doubts. She described feeling suffocated by everyone else's enthusiasm. John's parents were helping with the wedding preparations and started talking about how they couldn't wait to be grandparents.

Agnes decided to put the brakes on and moved out one weekend. She moved back in with her parents saying that she just needed time to herself. John was devastated and the relationship fell apart.

Agnes wasn't sure he was right for her any more. She felt that she had grown and changed and wanted different things to John. The thought of settling down at this point in time felt wrong to her.

When Agnes met George at the barbeque she felt a strong attraction to him and later described him as her soul mate. He understood her, didn't pressurise her and respected where she was coming from.

Her sisters were horrified. They made a lot of negative comments and were at pains to point out that he was just flattering himself with a younger woman – and having his cake and eating it because he didn't want more children. Agnes felt alone and unable to convince anyone of George's amazing qualities.

George

George had got married when he was 28 and had two daughters soon after. Looking back, he felt that he'd got married too soon and had a family before he was ready. He and his wife Sally had been drifting apart and it was she who had decided to divorce him. Sally had felt as though she and George were living more like brother and sister under the same roof than a married couple, and she wanted a more fulfilling relationship for herself. George had felt a growing emptiness as his daughters got older. He and Sally barely touched each other and sex between them happened very rarely. Sally and George did have some counselling, where George revealed that he felt that he got married too young and hadn't felt ready to be a father at the time when his daughters came along. He expressed that he'd lost his way and woke up one morning feeling as though life was passing him by.

When he encountered Agnes at the barbeque he admitted that he felt a huge spark of attraction. He saw her as a beautiful, vibrant woman with her whole life ahead of her.

He recognised that a relationship with Agnes would be very difficult for her parents to cope with, and he shared his concerns with a close friend of his. She warned him that he was walking into an emotional war zone and challenged him to think about whether Agnes was just his midlife crisis in progress as he tried to recapture his lost youth, or something more. This reaction shocked him.

Crunch Time

Agnes's parents felt very betrayed by her relationship with George and were livid with him. They had seen him as a family friend and as a father figure to Agnes. Psychologically Agnes's father found this difference very difficult to reconcile. He described George's motives as 'creepy' and worried that George was just using Agnes to boost his ego. Agnes's mother worried about how her daughter would deal with George's daughters and ex-wife Sally in this new context. She also knew that George didn't want any more children and was anxious that her daughter would be missing out on having a family of her own.

All these negative feelings and anxieties were projected on to Agnes and George, who felt overwhelmed by the negativity.

The Way Forward

Several weeks afterwards when the situation had calmed down and emotions weren't running as high, Agnes's parents invited them both for a meeting. They laid out their concerns and fears and told George that although they felt his intentions were good, they worried that he was in the relationship for all the wrong reasons. They felt that they knew him all too well – they knew how he had been in his first marriage because they had been confidants of both George and Sally. This caused them to worry deeply about his motives and thought that he was just having a life crisis.

Agnes expressed how she had always been 'their little girl' and felt that they treated her as if she was their prized possession and tried to control her, and because of this they couldn't see that she was her own person able to make up her own mind.

George and Agnes felt that they were committed to one another but knew that it would be a challenge to convince other people that they were together now.

It took time for each person to tolerate the situation and accept their relationship. Agnes's parents recognised that by being so critical in their reactions they were pushing her away from them. They recognised too that they had no control over the situation and had to let Agnes live her own life. They agreed to support her decision and be there whatever the outcome.

———

Self-Help Tips: Speaking To Your Family about Age Differences
When it comes to big age gaps in intimate relationships, family and friends are going to have opinions about it. Whether they express themselves openly or indirectly, you'll get to hear their views! That is why it is crucial to have a strategy for how to handle them.

1. It is important to speak to your own family first, without your partner, so that they have time to absorb what you are saying. Listen to the music behind the words. Are their fears and reactions based on an emotional over-reaction, because they believe that you are going against their expectations of you, or are their concerns and worries based on legitimate concerns?
2. Speak positively about your partner rather than apologise for them. Sometimes people try to appease family by saying, 'I know s/he isn't what you wanted, but …' This is a dangerous strategy as it gives your family permission to only focus on the negative.
3. If your family put up defensive walls and don't want to meet your partner at first, then keep the lines of communication open. Give them time to come around.
4. Be emotionally prepared for the introduction, it can be a fraught experience. Your parents, who may be of a similar age to your partner, could find it tricky. From their point of view they may be meeting a peer – this can raise discomfort levels and they may end up projecting their anxieties on

to your relationship. (Introducing your partner to your children is tackled in Chapter 7, Blended Families.)

5. Acknowledge that they may react badly. They may be genuinely concerned that being at different life stages will bring about real life challenges for you. Parents can also be totally wrong about who you should be with and may also disagree with one another.

6. You have to be prepared for the emotional ripple effect – friends, colleagues or acquaintances who may be ready to judge.

SEXUALITY

If you are lesbian, gay, bi or transgender, introducing your partner to your family may also involve coming out. Needless to say, this can be tough. Families can have so many different reactions to their child's sexuality. There are some who are fortunate enough to have families who are able to accept and integrate not only you but your partner into the fabric of the family. But others may not be so fortunate.

If your family are in the dark about your sexuality, then deciding to kill two birds with one stone and introducing your partner and your sexuality at the same time is likely to be explosive.

It is so important that you protect and prepare yourself for the emotional fall-out. Even the most loving parents may respond with disappointment. Why? Because living in a heterosexually skewed world, most parents make the assumption that their kids are straight. It also goes back to their core beliefs about you, their hopes and dreams for you and their fear about the reaction of others.

Self-Help Tips: Coming Out to Your Family

1. Do they need to be told in a more direct manner or very gradually? Even if they suspect you're gay, they'll still be

shocked and upset. So figure out a way to tell them that will give them the space to get their intense feelings out. If face to face is too hard, it is fine to write a letter, email or call them.

2. If you are aware your family have been playing hide and seek with your sexuality, then they have decided what they can't see doesn't exist for them. You may have colluded in this scenario in order to avoid hurting their feelings. But inevitably hiding everything under the rug creates a massive emotional tripping hazard. It might be so tempting to get it over and done with, but resist this approach. First, rehearse on your own or with a trusted friend exactly what you want to say.

3. Prepare yourself emotionally for the potential fallout. Remember their reaction may be wrapped up in fear and anxiety rather than spite and horror.

4. Have someone supportive to talk to and give you a hug afterwards, especially if your parents take it badly.

5. You may find it helpful to sit down with your parents separately and be honest with them.

6. Getting extra help and support from professional bodies could really help you too. There are plenty of organisations who offer excellent advice, see Further Help on pages 271–4.

———

Case Study: Family Strife

Zoe (30) and Michelle (32) had been living together for a year. They'd met at work where they were both teachers, and started living together after a few months. Their relationship had had its ups and downs, but on the whole they described their relationship as a happy one. However, Zoe was alienated from her family and so had never introduced them to Michelle.

Zoe

Zoe was the youngest of four – two older brothers and one sister. Both her parents were very involved in the local church community and her father was a lay preacher. Her mother had retired early from her career in nursing due to ill health. The family were popular and very well known in their Afro-Caribbean community.

Zoe had always felt that she had a sexual preference for women, and when she was 17 had opened up to her older sister Jo who was 19 at the time. She'd asked Jo to keep it a secret from her parents. Jo hadn't been very supportive. She accused Zoe of being her usual dramatic self to get attention and said that she'd grow out of it. However, in one heated row with her parents about her own boyfriend that their parents didn't approve of, Jo blurted out Zoe's secret. This caused a huge family fight and Zoe was told by her father to move out.

This rejection cut very deep. Her whole family behaved as though she no longer existed. She had to deal with moving from being at the centre of a positive family and community support system that was loving and accepting to being alone and feeling betrayed and excluded.

Zoe had spent a number of years working to heal these wounds, and had had therapy to come to terms with the void that she'd felt at the painful loss of her whole family. She often expressed how hard it was to know that they were alive and well but choosing not to reach out to her. She had never really shared the depth of loss she'd felt with anyone, until she'd met Michelle.

Zoe received a letter from her mother one day informing her of her father's death, details of when the funeral was and a request to attend. This shocking news had left Zoe in emotional turmoil and grief.

Michelle

Michelle had one younger sister. She described her family as fairly ordinary. Her father was a builder and her mother ran her own child-minding business from home and occasionally worked at the local primary school as a classroom assistant. Michelle felt forced to come out to her parents when she was 16 after her mother confronted her about rumours that Michelle had been spotted kissing a girl. This had caused a storm of fury at home. Her mother expressed her *embarrassment and shame, focusing on how people around would now judge her as a bad mother, incapable of bringing her own family up properly. Michelle's father gave her the silent treatment for several weeks.*

It took a long time for the family to come to terms with Michelle's sexuality and more often than not they kept her at arm's length. They didn't really want to hear her news and kept conversations light when they were all together. Once Michelle had started working and created a life for herself she saw her parents less and less, and they almost always declined invitations to her home.

Crunch Time
Both Michelle and Zoe had faced difficult family issues. But when Zoe got the letter from her mother about her father's death and funeral she wasn't sure how to react. Her grief was filled with anger that she had effectively been airbrushed out of the family. But she also felt the deep loss of her father whom she'd been very close to while growing up.

Zoe wanted to go to the funeral and wanted Michelle to be with her by her side. Michelle, on the other hand, felt that this was a really bad idea as it could cause so much more trouble than it was worth.

The Way Forward
Zoe decided to have a couple of counselling sessions to work out what she should do. This helped her to understand the deeper issues at play: like the family losses that both she and Michelle had experienced as a result of being open and honest about who they were as people. Through this process she recognised that Michelle may have been fearful about replaying her own family script – and being treated once again as someone who a family was ashamed of.

They decided to take things slowly. They travelled to the funeral together and Zoe attended the funeral on her own. She reached out to her mother and asked her if she wanted to meet her partner. Zoe's mother reluctantly agreed.

They met a few days later at the local bed and breakfast where Zoe and Michelle were staying. Zoe's mother was able to acknowledge how happy her daughter was with her partner and, although still clearly uncomfortable with her sexuality, she was able to appreciate that her daughter's partner made her happy. She expressed guilt that somehow she'd done something wrong to Zoe growing up to 'make her gay' and described how her father prayed for her happiness and hoped his daughter would turn back to the right path. Zoe, in turn, reflected on her father's favourite saying which was 'to always be true to yourself' and how ironic it was that because of his words she was now living an authentic life.

Michelle had made the decision to keep a polite relationship with her family who she'd conceded would never really be able to deal with her sexuality. She was more reconciled within herself about her family's limitations.

It took many months of very small steps for Zoe to start reconnecting with her family and she knew things would never be the same as in her childhood, but she was able to move on from the wounds from her past.

———

CLASS CONFLICT

If you and your partner come from different class backgrounds, your family or your partner's family may hold negative beliefs about the differing class. This may be based on a number of factors: negative experiences, long-held beliefs that have been passed down from others and/or having very little personal experience with people from different class backgrounds and therefore basing their beliefs on what they've seen, heard or read about from a distance. This can make introducing your partner an uncomfortable experience if you haven't prepared them.

Self-Help Tips: Different Class Backgrounds and Your Family
1. Be honest and recognise that you can't just separate yourself or your partner from family – close or not, their

impact and influence is far-reaching. Hoping that family influence will disappear the longer you're together is an unrealistic expectation. So, first of all, be honest with your partner about your family's views.

2. Talk to your family about how important your partner is to you and ask them to assume nothing and to be open.

3. Ask your family to compromise and meet you halfway. Give them permission to find out about your partner by inviting them to ask honest and fair questions, instead of staying quiet and sticking to stereotypes. This will give them the chance to get to know your partner first-hand, before making up their minds.

4. It's important that you and your partner always have each other's backs. If family or certain family members continue to treat your partner and your relationship inappropriately, then it is important to reiterate to them that they need to respect your relationship. If they don't, then make it clear that you will have to limit the amount of time you spend with them in order to protect your relationship.

5. If there are other members of the family who are positive towards your relationship, then enlist their support in handling more negative reactions from other family members.

———

Case Study: The Wrong Class

Stacey (27) and Jack (26) had grown up in the same local community and attended the same primary and secondary schools. They had been casual friends, but hadn't seen each other for several years when they connected again in their mid-twenties on Facebook. They arranged to meet up the next time that they were both visiting their parents.

When they finally met up again, they found that they had a deep connection and were strongly attracted to each other. They started dating and after six months Jack invited Stacey over to his parents' house for dinner.

Jack told his parents that he wanted them to meet his girlfriend but he wouldn't say who she was because he wanted to surprise them. Jack felt that his parents would be very happy for him, because, as he remembers it, they adored Stacey when she was younger and always said nice things about her.

Dinner appeared to go very well from Jack's point of view: his parents seemed to be warm and interested in what Stacey was doing, but once she'd left their disapproval poured out. His mother described Stacey as nice enough, but not for him. She made it clear that she hoped that this relationship was nothing serious to him as she strongly believed that Stacey just wanted a relationship with Jack in order to climb up the social ladder and better herself.

Jack was absolutely horrified at the prejudice coming from his parents – particularly his mother. (He knew that his father was often persuaded by his more domineering mother when it came to more domestic matters.) Jack desperately wanted his parents' approval and, although he knew his parents had certain elitist views, hadn't expected such snobbery.

Jack

Jack was the youngest of three brothers. All three had followed in their father's footsteps and worked in the financial industry. Jack's brothers were both married and lived abroad. The family had core beliefs about the importance of status, money and power. Jack's father believed that women should be properly educated in order to stay at home and raise their family to the highest standard. Jack's mother also held similar beliefs and had come from a very wealthy and educated background. She'd given up working as soon as her children came along and prided herself in raising them properly.

When Jack was a toddler, his father lost a very lucrative contract and the family faced a tough time. They couldn't afford three sets of boarding school fees and made what was for them a difficult decision to send Jack to the local primary until things improved. Jack loved his school and made a lot of friends. At the end of primary school he decided that he wanted to go to the local secondary with his friends. His parents' situation had by then improved and they'd signed him up for a boarding school. Jack was sent away to school against his will, and there he showed signs of acute distress. He found the emotional and physical separation from his family and his friends incredibly difficult. He made several attempts to run away and the headmaster finally recommended that the school wasn't suitable for him. Jack went back home and attended the local secondary school where he felt much happier.

Jack's mother had struggled to come to terms with her drop in status when Jack was at primary school. She carried very set ideas about her identity and befriending other parents at the school was very hard for her. It was because of Jack's amiable nature that his mother got to meet so many people. He was very popular and was often invited to parties and sleepovers. It was during this time that Jack and Stacey's mothers encountered each other at the school gates. They became acquaintances but certainly weren't friends.

Jack and Stacey were part of the same friendship group and often spent time together. Stacey had been to Jack's house many times and on the surface his mother had always been very welcoming of her. This is the memory Jack retained of the relationship between his family and Stacey.

Stacey

Stacey was the eldest of three sisters. She was the first member of her family to go university and had a successful career in public relations. She described her family as hard-working, warm and loving. Her father worked in construction and her mother was a doctor's receptionist. Her parents had always had educational aspirations for her and encouraged her to believe in her abilities. When Stacey was at primary school, her parents got divorced and a couple of years later her mother had remarried. Stacey's mother had become the subject of much gossip in the local community and Stacey was often teased and picked on by other children. She developed a very tough exterior, but often felt isolated and different. Jack and she became friends around this time. He was very sensitive to her feelings and would often defend her against bullies.

Stacey had always been very aware of the differences between her family and Jack's family. Her mother sometimes talked about the snobby attitudes coming from Jack's parents.

When Stacey told her mother that she was now dating Jack, Stacey's mother was very shocked and surprised. She remembered Jack as a loving, sensitive boy, but with awful cold parents! Jack had already met Stacey's mother again and she'd welcomed him with open arms. He had always felt welcome in their home while growing up and had formed a strong attachment to Stacey's family.

Stacey had expressed concern about meeting his parents, but Jack had reassured her that they would be really happy to see her again. Stacey's mother warned her that the meeting could be fraught, but Stacey trusted Jack's feelings on this.

Crunch Time

Jack's idealised view of reintroducing Stacey as his girlfriend had been crushed and he felt embarrassed about their attitudes. Stacey felt that the meeting with his parents had gone okay, but sensed that his parents really didn't approve of her. There had been several references made to Jack's ex-girlfriend who had gone off and married someone else because Jack was dithering about. Jack's father had jokingly asked Stacey how many times her mother had now been married – this dig wasn't lost on Stacey.

It appeared as though Jack's parents had selective memory and only wanted to focus on negative events in Stacey's life.

The Way Forward

Stacey quickly realised that there was little chance of Jack's parents ever approving of her as his girlfriend even though she knew that he was more different than similar to the rest of his family. Jack felt torn by his family's reactions. He hoped that they would accept Stacey as his girlfriend because she made him happy.

It was through having some counselling that Jack was able to confront some of the difficult feelings he had about his own family. He realised that his family had very rigid thinking about other people and were emotionally very avoidant. Growing up, his needs and feelings were seldom considered, and he saw now how he often attached himself to other people's families in order to feel affection. He had felt an affinity with Stacey and her family from a very young age, and felt loved and accepted by them all.

He recognised that he had developed 'magic thinking' in order to protect himself from difficult feelings and that his survival strategy in life had always been to hope for the best.

Stacey and Jack continued to date for a while, and although their relationship did eventually fizzle out, they remained good friends. Jack recognised that he needed to get to grips with his past and develop a healthy relationship with himself, in order to have healthy relationships in future. His relationship with Stacey had been the catalyst for this emotional change. Stacey realised that she had reconnected with Jack at a vulnerable time when she needed familiarity and security. She also learnt an important truth about herself from the experience, in that she wasn't willing to compromise who she was as a person in order to belong to a family that didn't accept that.

––––––

There are many factors to consider when introducing your partner and your family to one another and it may at times feel like an emotional roller coaster. But just like any other relationship, it takes time to build a meaningful and lasting connection, find out likes and dislikes, discover where the boundaries lie, as well as to learn how to effectively communicate with one other. When your partner and your family matter to you, then it is important to acknowledge that this is an ongoing process, which needs loving commitment, time and sometimes patience from everyone in order to reap the positive benefits.

Chapter 3
Let's Live Together

I met a couple at a party a few years ago, who, after a few glasses of wine, shared with me that they'd been 'stuck' living together for 15 years. He expressed rather grumpily how she'd just 'crept up' on him and moved herself in. She laughed this off, and then described how, after all this time, she still only had one drawer at his house that she could call her own and that, apart from a teapot, she hadn't been allowed to contribute to buying any of the furniture in the house!

They beautifully illustrated to me how 'accidentally living together' can have two people stagger on unhappily for years: possibly through fear, lack of motivation to change things or simply convenience – because they just didn't have an honest conversation early on in their relationship. Their reactive approach had led to years of feeling that they had no choice but to be stuck together.

Considering a deeper commitment is a very big deal and needs careful thought, and if, like the couple at the party, 'it just happens', then the relationship may be in for a very bumpy ride.

It is very easy to simply slide into what seems like the next logical step. You're in love, you have so much in common, you spend most of your time with each other – why not just set up home together?

And sometimes having to tackle those nitty-gritty relationship questions with your partner can feel harder than having root canal – so we avoid doing it.

A step-by-step approach to considering a deeper commitment is a very smart move. I know this may sound very planned – after all where is the spontaneity in that? But without some kind of understanding of what you're getting into, you may end up in a situation you feel bound to stick with – rather than ensuring that you are making positive choices based on how you both feel about the relationship.

Moving in together will at some point bring into sharp focus your core beliefs and values. Without a clear understanding of how you or your partner feels there is always the potential to add stress to the relationship.

ISSUES TO CONSIDER

There are basic issues that couples often don't talk about in the early stages, which can become bigger problems further down the line – these include:

1. An understanding of what you both mean by commitment. You may be in it for the long haul and assume your partner is on the same page – but they may not be.
2. Where you stand on issues of money and finances. This is another key area that can cause major conflict further down the line if it is not discussed. For instance – if you're the saver and they are the spender, or considering whether to have a joint account. These differences can throw up areas of potential conflict.
3. How much time you want to spend together and apart. Once you're under the same roof, you may assume that you and your partner will do everything together – however, they may have very different ideas.

4. Are you ready for this step? Everyone else is moving in together, so why don't we? The pressure to follow what your social group do, or what your family suggest, could add stress to your decision.

These are key issues that you and your partner *need* to think about and then discuss together when considering a deeper commitment.

QUICK COMMITMENT QUIZ

A great way to open up a conversation about these issues is to go through the following questions. Take some time out when you're feeling relaxed, answer them independently as honestly as you can, then sit down together and discuss your responses and how you both feel about taking the next step.

1. When you think of a deeper commitment, what does it mean to you personally? For instance:

➤ A monogamous relationship that lasts a lifetime.
➤ Living together for a while to see where things take you.
➤ A trial run before marriage.
➤ An open relationship, but living under one roof.

2. When you think about money, what comes to mind?

➤ Money is for spending now.
➤ Money is essentially for saving for the future.
➤ Money gives you freedom to do what you want.
➤ Money gives you a sense of security.
➤ Separate, independent bank accounts with a joint account for bills and mortgage payments.

➤ Separate, independent bank accounts where you take it in turn to pay bills, etc.
➤ To have joint bank accounts for everything.

3. Moving in together means:
➤ Spending the majority of your free time together.
➤ Spending some time together and some time with your own friends.
➤ Living like flatmates.
➤ Someone to share the bills and household chores with.
➤ A ready-made social life.
➤ Your partner will take care of you financially.
➤ You are going to take care of your partner financially.

4. Living together at this point in my life means:
➤ Starting a family at some point in the future.
➤ Deciding to stay together and agreeing not to have children.
➤ Seeing whether the relationship works out or not.
➤ Convenience – because you hate being alone at the moment.
➤ Because you need to find a new place to live anyway.

5. What thoughts and feelings come into your mind when you imagine yourself making the move to live together?

6. Make a list of three things that you feel excited about and three things that you're worried about.

7. Name three moving-in priorities: e.g. we must have a joint account, we must have two holidays a year.

8. Name three moving-in 'nice to haves': e.g. it would be nice to go out twice a week as a couple, it would be nice to spend one weekend a month away with my friends without my partner.

9. Are there other factors that may influence your decision to make a deeper commitment? Perhaps:

➤ Your family members constantly dropping hints about the two of you moving in together.

➤ Your parents are asking you about when they'll be grandparents.

➤ All your friends are settling down and you're the last one to do this.

➤ You are feeling under pressure to start a family before it's too late.

➤ Your partner is persuading you that this is what you both want.

After answering these questions for yourself and then sharing your responses with your partner, you will have a clearer idea of your personal and joint values and beliefs, as well as a clear insight into your motives for wanting to live together.

If you now both feel that moving in together is right for you, then that's fantastic. However, if these questions have thrown up some differences in opinion, or doubts, then it is vital to discuss them further.

COMMITMENT CONCERNS

Making a commitment, for some people, can be one of the most difficult issues to tackle. You may like the idea of commitment, but when it comes to the reality of it, feel like running away. There a number of factors that can affect your decision to make a full commitment. The atmosphere you grew up in may influence your beliefs about commitment. For instance, coming from a family where relationships between parents weren't stable or long lasting, may lead you to believe that relationships can't go the distance, and as a result, you may view living together as a temporary state. Or you may have commitment issues because of previous negative experiences – like being hurt or badly let down. In some other instances, not feeling financially secure enough to commit may prevent you from taking that step. Developing your awareness of what commitment means to you, and what may be getting in the way and influencing your decision, is crucial to ensuring that you make the right decision for you.

———

Case Study: Push Me–Pull You

Tom (35) and Beth (29) had been together for four years. They'd met at a work conference. Both of them were care managers at different foster care homes, and they lived some distance apart. They'd found that they had a lot in common and both felt deeply passionate about the work that they did. They made great efforts to meet regularly and the first two years of the relationship were very happy. Beth eventually applied for a transfer and moved closer to Tom. She bought her own place and they carried on seeing each other.

They spent many holidays and Christmases together, which Beth almost always organised and Tom was happy to fit in with. Beth had often dropped hints about wanting to start a family, but Tom never really responded. She found this so frustrating, and often complained to her friends that he was unresponsive. Tom's mother often hinted that the two of them should get married and settle down, she was desperate to be a grandmother – and, as her only child, Tom was her only hope.

Beth had had one previous long-term relationship, which simply fizzled out after a few years. She'd spent a couple of years on her own before meeting Tom and felt very clear in her own mind about what she wanted from her next relationship. In Tom, she felt that she'd found someone who she had a lot in common with. The work they did reflected this and they had similar views about bringing up children. Often when Tom had had a bit too much to drink, he'd share with her his desire to have a big family with her and his dreams about moving out of the town and into the country so he could have lots of animals too. Beth would feel positive and lifted when she heard this, but, more often than not, a few days later, when she'd bring the conversation round to the future, he'd just change the subject.

Tom had previously had two long-term relationships. One when he was 18 – a woman whom he described as the love of his life – that ended when he was 23, and another when he was 25, which lasted for six years. Tom actually didn't like being on his own. In between long-term relationships, he'd had short-term flings.

He knew that he raised Beth's hopes whenever he talked about the future. He loved having her around, but didn't feel quite ready to join their lives together. He wanted her – and he didn't want her. Every time he felt that she got too close, he'd push her away, and if she distanced herself from him, he'd pull her right back. This push–pull dynamic was a feature of their relationship.

Tom

Tom was an only child who'd had difficulties growing up. His father was often away working and was also emotionally absent from his son. When Tom was a very small child, he spent a lot of time with his mother. He struggled to fit in at school and often felt misunderstood and an outsider. His mother decided to send him to boarding school at the age of eight on the advice of a family friend, who suggested that he needed to be among other children and in a more regulated environment. Tom wasn't asked if he'd like to go, he was told one morning over breakfast. His mother was very matter of fact about it, and Tom was told not to cry because he was going on a special adventure.

Tom described the first few years at boarding school as deeply painful. He longed to go home and he ran away a few times, which got him into more trouble. He hated being among so many boys and longed to have his own space. At the same time as he longed to be with his mother, he also felt so much rage towards her because she'd sent him away from her. He eventually learnt to stifle his deepest feelings. However, his rage was never far away and this manifested itself as passive-aggressiveness.

With Beth his avoidance played out in his strong resistance to commit to her and the confusing message he often gave her – of wanting his freedom, yet wanting her there for him. He subconsciously frustrated her at every turn.

Beth

Beth was the eldest of two sisters and grew up in a small country village. Her parents ran the local post office and were the centre of the local community. She described her upbringing as very normal – she attended the local school, had lots of friends and felt very grounded. She saw her future as settling down eventually and having a big family.

When she'd met Tom she saw in him someone who was loving and caring and nurturing. This was very evident in the passion he showed for the work he did at the children's foster care home. The relationship from her point of view had been very content and happy for the first two years, but she experienced growing anxiety about Tom's lack of response in taking the relationship to a deeper level.

She had never really challenged his treatment of her and had allowed a lot of his frustrating behaviour towards her to simply slide. He had been very open with her about his childhood and she felt very strongly that with love and nurturance from her she would be able to offer him the security and trusting bond he so desperately craved.

Crunch Time

However, after four years, Beth decided enough was enough and she issued Tom with an ultimatum. Either they moved in together and made a commitment to each other or the relationship had to end. Beth recognised that she had spent a lot of time trying to work Tom out. She'd become consumed by his problems and had prioritised his feelings over her own. She had gone from being someone who had a very secure picture of herself, to a person who doubted herself a lot of the time. She began to see herself through Tom's eyes: needy, nagging and clingy. She was tired of spending her energy reassuring him or absorbing his anger, or being a parental figure who organised his life for him. She was fed up with being stuck in a draining vicious cycle.

Tom felt guilty about his treatment of her, but had continued to play out his distancing wound from the past. The shock of her finally speaking up brought him into her reality. He could no longer maintain his perception that it was all Beth's fault, and he knew deep down that stubbornly viewing the relationship this way gave him permission to remain angry and keep Beth at arm's length.

The Way Forward

Tom recognised that he needed to learn an appropriate strategy to manage his anger. He had counselling on his own that focused on his pain from the past. He began to see that he had serious trust issues, which would continue to affect his relationship with Beth if he didn't address them.

Beth saw that by remaining unassertive with Tom, and effectively taking on the role of a loving parent, she'd lost her own identity and become anxious and frustrated. She realised that she needed to be more direct and honest with him and speak her truth.

They both decided that while Tom was going through his therapy they would continue to see each other, but wait before they moved in together. They agreed to review regularly how they were both feeling. This also helped Beth to refocus on her own needs and regain her self-confidence.

DISCOVER YOUR COMMITMENT LEVELS

It is so important to have your expectations about commitment all straightened out in your own head first when thinking about taking the relationship to the next commitment level. This will help you to assert yourself and speak up for what you need. Ask yourself:

➤ Do I want to live with you because I just don't want to be alone any more?

➤ Is living together for me really about commitment or convenience?

➤ Will you support me if I really need you?

➤ Will I support you if you really need me to?

➤ Do I see us living together as me having someone to look after me?

➤ Does living together mean me looking after you?

➤ Am I happy to live anywhere with you, or will moving out of my comfort zone cause problems?

Working through these questions will help you to more clearly understand your motivation for wanting to take the relationship to the next level, and whether this is the best way forward for you and for your partner.

THE MONEY CHAT

Money and financial issues come high on a list of things that couples tend to argue about.

With this in mind, rather than hoping this will never be an issue in your relationship, it is vital to have an honest discussion about money when you are thinking of moving in together. This will ensure that you both have an understanding of each other's values, feelings and spending habits, as well as the opportunity to plan how you both intend to share bills, or what you want to spend money on, for example.

Talking about money is an incredibly emotional topic. It can bring up issues from your past, that you may not have even realised were connected to money. Whether you're moving in to see how things go and renting a flat together, or deciding that you are in this relationship for the long haul, it is never too soon in a relationship to talk about it. If left unacknowledged, conversations about money can become an embittered battleground at any time ...

YOUR MONEY SCRIPT

We all develop what I like to call a money script. Your money script is: your attitude to money, what value you place on it and how you feel, think and behave when it comes to money. Your money script matters in your relationship because it affects all aspects of the dynamic, from basic practicalities like who buys the loo-roll, or who pays for a night out, to whether to have a joint account or not. Your money script may be shaped and influenced by the messages you grew up with and the attitudes that your parents or primary caregivers had towards money. So for one person money may mean power or control, and for the other it may mean freedom or security. It is important to identify the messages you internalised about the value of money.

> **QUICK MONEY HEALTH CHECK**
> Do this quick exercise with your partner to work out your money script.
>
> ➤ Are you essentially 'now focused' when it comes to money? This means – thinking that life is for living

in the moment, so if you see something you like your tendency is to buy it now, you are an impulse shopper.

You prefer to spend rather than save.

➤ Are you essentially 'future focused' when it comes to money? This means – you like to put money away for a rainy day, you prefer to compare prices before you buy, you can delay purchasing something.

You prefer to save rather than spend.

➤ Put a figure on what monthly income for you equates to:

1. Being well off.
2. Being okay.
3. Feeling the pinch.

(For example, Jill's monthly amount for feeling well off is an income of £3,000. Steve's monthly amount for feeling well off is an income of £1,500.)

Becoming aware of how similar or different you and your partner are when it comes to being 'now focused' or 'future focused', will help you to understand where potential money conflicts may arise from. Developing this level of understanding with each other is an important first step in helping you to minimise money rows. The next step is to check whether you and your partner have put down similar amounts for what different monthly incomes equate to. Then discuss with each other why you have chosen these particular amounts, and notice what you have each based your chosen amounts on. For instance: lifestyle, rent, eating out, saving money, luxuries, holidays and so on. This will help you clearly see where your views on money differ and where they are similar, so that you can start thinking about what amount would help you *both* to feel secure.

Case Study: My Money, Your Money, Our Money

Joseph (28) and Susie (29) felt that they were ready to move in together after dating for two years. They felt that they'd been through the first flush of the honeymoon period and were still very much in love. They often talked about a future together, but not in any great detail. They spent most weekends at each other's flats and both felt that maybe it was time to set up home together.

For Joseph living together not only meant living with the woman he was deeply in love with, but it also meant saving a lot of time and money by being under one roof. Susie loved Joseph very much and she saw living together as a sign that they were in the relationship for the long haul – for her it meant marriage and starting a family. They never really discussed the nitty-gritty of what their individual hopes and expectations were.

Crunch Time

Disagreements soon flared up when Joseph assumed Susie would sell her flat and move into his flat because, as he saw it, his flat was a better practical solution – it was bigger and closer to all the local amenities. He had it all planned out. He felt that he had the more stable job in personnel management and so he told her that she would put the money from the sale of her flat into a joint savings account and the two of them could then save towards buying a bigger place within two years. Susie had other ideas. She worked as a freelance caterer and had been used to managing her own money and had her own financial arrangements in place. She wanted them both to sell their respective flats and start afresh on an equal footing as a couple in their new home. Both dug their heels in and fought hard to persuade the other to come round to their way of thinking.

Susie had always had a strong, outspoken voice and had no trouble expressing her needs very clearly – she had a tendency to be the dominant voice. She was an only child who had been brought up by parents who encouraged her to be independent and go for what she wanted. For Susie her flat symbolised all this – it was hers, she chose it and she owned it. Feeling as though she had to give it up in order to move in with Joseph felt like giving up her independence. She saw buying a place together as a compromise and as a symbol of real commitment and equal sharing.

Joseph had almost always approached life logically. He was also an only child, brought up in a single-parent family. His mother was very aware of being careful with money and emphasised the importance of never wasting any resources, Joseph strongly felt that he had to have control of the money and work towards making wise financial decisions.

Of course, none of these issues had really arisen before, so they'd never really had the tough conversation about where to live, how they'd divide money or even what their beliefs and values were about living together.

Although Susie and Joseph were committed to one another in principle, in practice they hadn't really tested this out. After much arguing, they decided to seek support to break the stalemate. They booked an appointment with a counsellor.

Susie

During the counselling sessions, Susie recognised that she had reacted powerfully to being infantilised by Joseph. She described not having a voice in this important decision and worried that this was going to be a recurring pattern in their relationship. She also began to see that she didn't really want to hear Joseph's point of view – and had simply been shouting him down. After exploring this a little further, she admitted that the thought of giving up her home to live with Joseph had felt stressful to her and had left her feeling as though she was giving up her identity as a strong, independent and capable woman. Her response was to stand her ground, perceive Joseph as the enemy – and protest loudly from her corner.

Joseph

Joseph recognised that he'd assumed the parental role and admitted that he did sometimes talk to Susie as if she were a child because he worried about losing control of the finances. He saw her career as wonderful but saw her as financially erratic – and didn't like the way she seemed to spend money on frivolities. He subconsciously resolved to protect them both from imagined disaster by taking charge of the money. Exploring this a little deeper, Joseph revealed to Susie for the first time that his father had had a gambling problem when Joseph was very young. The family had been in serious debt and had almost lost their family home. Joseph's mother had had to work two jobs to stabilise the family finances. Joseph remembers very clearly the feelings of helplessness and anxiety that he grew up with, as well as an atmosphere of grave uncertainty. After bailing his father out many times, Joseph's mother finally had enough and divorced him. Joseph grew up feeling he needed to stay in total control of money in order to feel secure. He carried a deep-seated fear that if he ever lost control of money, he would end up like his father.

They recognised that they both did want to live together and had to find a way to compromise that suited them both. Their desire to stay fiercely independent had left no room to develop a couples' script that included the art of give and take at its very core.

The Way Forward

By discussing their specific expectations and concerns up front and in a neutral environment, Susie and Joseph were better equipped to discuss what the best way forward for them was – as a couple, which encompassed both their financial and emotional needs.

Joseph's breakthrough moment occurred when he had to consider what would happen if – due to unforeseen circumstances – Susie had to support him financially in future. This challenge to his rigid life script helped Joseph recognise that his inflexible approach could scupper their relationship. For Susie her moment of realisation came when she recognised that refusing to listen to Joseph had prevented him from sharing his deeper anxieties about money and that allowing him to be more open enabled them both to feel more equal in the relationship.

They recognised the importance of give and take, as well as mutual respect in how they communicated their concerns to one another. They both realised that they had fiercely independent streaks – and that a healthy relationship needed a mixture of independence as well as flexibility in order to create a balanced approach.

With the help of counselling, they were able to work towards a joint agreement. Susie decided to move in with Joseph, as she recognised that this did make practical and financial sense. They agreed to maintain separate current accounts and decided to open a joint account that they would both contribute to in order to pay the mortgage and for other household goods. They agreed to have monthly money updates in order to ensure that they were both happy with how things were going.

———

Self-Help Tips: Handling Joint Money
1. Try to take emotion out of the conversation and approach it like a business meeting, so that you and your partner can undertake the money chat as one adult to another (and therefore avoid it descending into an emotional bust-up).
2. Make a joint-money budget, so that you can create a straightforward and clear picture of how money would be handled.
3. Agreeing to keep each other regularly updated regarding money will prevent unnecessary arguments and help prevent keeping money secrets from each other.
4. If you are able to, deciding to have individual accounts can give you both independence and a sense of personal control and security.
5. By ring-fencing an amount to put away each month in a joint account for food, bills, special occasions and the mortgage you can keep money boundaried and under control.

BOUNDARIES

Setting boundaries is a vital skill for creating and maintaining a healthy and balanced relationship. Being clear about what you will and will not tolerate, and being honest about what makes you feel anxious or uncomfortable, enables you to understand and then articulate what your limits are. Speaking your truth will ensure that you avoid a build-up of resentment in the future.

Different people will have different tolerance levels. You may be fine with your mum having a spare key to your home, but your partner may not. Your partner may be fine with sharing intimate details of your relationship with his family, but you may find this a breach of trust.

When boundaries are vague or non-existent, you may both be left feeling as though you are being taken for granted, or being manipulated into living according to someone else's needs and wants. You may even end up ignoring your own needs and putting up with a situation that you would not stand for if it was anybody else; just to keep the relationship on an even keel.

Ignoring concerns in order to fit in with someone else is a recipe for future tensions. For example, imagine not telling your partner that you can't stand it when he puts the lights on and watches TV in bed after you've gone to sleep! It may not have been something that seemed a big deal at first, but the longer it continues the more you may end up feeling angry and resentful.

———

Case Study: Under Pressure

John (37) and Karen (29) had been together three years. They met at work, when John joined a small firm of architects where Karen worked as a PA. This was a family-run business and was owned by Karen's father; it had a close-knit and friendly atmosphere. Karen's brother and sister-in-law also worked there, and they often socialised as a team outside of work. John enjoyed his job and saw his relationship with Karen as perfect.

John was quickly integrated into Karen's family and he experienced them as wonderful people who truly loved each other, and he liked the way that they spent every Sunday together for family lunches. Karen was equally delighted that John fitted in so easily with her family and she felt relieved that the family tradition of weekend gatherings would continue and include John from now on. They planned to move in together and the whole family were delighted.

However, after three years of spending nearly every weekend with Karen's family, as well as every working day with some of them, John was experiencing a growing sense of frustration, and he began to have serious doubts about wanting to move in with Karen. He felt stifled and had had enough! But he didn't speak up because he felt guilty, and worried that he would lose his job if he rocked the boat. The longer things went on, the more resentful he became. Instead of sharing this with Karen, he just became sulkier every weekend. Feeling defensive, Karen accused him of behaving like his dad – distant and moody.

John

John wanted to understand where his feelings of frustration were coming from, and so he started a journal. He focused first on his relationship history. It became clear from his perceptions of his current relationship, family, friends and past relationships that there was a pattern of interaction emerging. He noticed that he formed attachments based on his need for approval from significant others, usually at great cost to his own feelings and needs. An exploration of the relationship with his parents gave a clearer picture of his early experiences.

John was an only child who always craved the love and attention of his father, but found that his mother's forceful presence meant that his father usually met her needs first and John faded into the background feeling rejected. This early three-way relationship *seemed to have informed how John behaved in his relationships. He often felt as though he was battling to get approval – whether it was in friendships, relationships or at work – but what he felt almost always happened to him was that someone else more important than him always got there first.*

In relationships, in order to attract love his way, John seems to have internalised his father's beliefs and ways of behaving. He became keenly aware of the needs of others and often put their needs first before his own. Although as an adult John rarely saw or spoke to his parents, his desire to belong to a family played out in other relationships. He became desperate to quickly attach himself to other people's families – whether it was friends or girlfriends, and, although he was often included as one of the family, he felt that he never truly belonged and could be thrown out at any time. Eventually, all relationships did appear to end badly for him. John's anxiety to fit in, and lack of assertiveness, culminated in a self-fulfilling prophecy – more often than not he was rejected.

Karen

Karen was brought up in a very close-knit family. She was the youngest of three children and had two older brothers. She described her family as very traditional with her father as head of the family. Her father was very protective of his 'little girl' and instructed her brothers to protect her and look after her at all times. Karen described her relationship with her mother as very close – and felt that they were like best friends.

When she was a teenager Karen described how she often sought out her family's approval about who to date and who to be friends with. Karen was very used to getting her material and emotional needs met by her family members. Her father bought her her first car, gave her a job in the family business and he was poised to buy her her first home whenever she decided that she wanted to settle down. Her mother was always there to discuss everything in great detail with her. She didn't question her family's involvement in all aspects of her life; she enjoyed the closeness and wanted them to approve of whatever she was up to.

Crunch Time

Things came to a head when one evening Karen told John that her mother had found them a lovely two-bedroom cottage only half a mile from the family home. She thought that this would really make John happy. In an uncharacteristic outburst, John aggressively expressed how he didn't want to live with her any more. He told her how emasculated he felt by her deferring every decision to her family, instead of discussing things with him. He was so angry with her because, as he saw it, she didn't even think that he needed a say in where they lived.

Karen revealed to him how anxious she was about upsetting her family, whom she felt she owed a lot to – and she admitted feeling that she'd be letting her family down if she branched out and moved away. However, she also told John that she liked how close her family were – and that being involved in each other's lives felt normal and comforting to her.

John suggested that they needed help to sort their feelings out, but Karen thought this was unnecessary. She suggested that they had a family meeting instead. She told her family what their problems were, to which the response was utter surprise. They were unable to see why John was being so hostile.

John realised that things were getting out of hand and work was becoming very uncomfortable, so he made the difficult decision to leave. This created a crisis for Karen and she agreed to have counselling.

The Way Forward

Over the course of six months, they had counselling both individually and as a couple.

Karen realised that the entwined relationship with her family had left her being overly dependent on them and as a result she was scared to make decisions for herself. She was also able to admit that she was anxious about separating from her family and feared becoming lonely and isolated.

John undertook a simple but powerful exercise which led to a breakthrough in his understanding of his own identity and behaviour. He drew a family portrait where he placed his parents at the centre, surrounded by a circle, and he placed himself outside of this circle. Asked to draw previous relationships, and his current relationship with Karen, the portrait was the same. He always put himself outside of the family circle. This image helped John to understand more clearly how he continued to recreate his early wound, and how his need to belong and his fear of rejection often meant that he felt that he didn't have the right to assert himself.

Karen

Karen worked on small, manageable steps to separating from her family and putting boundaries in place. The counsellor prepared Karen for the possibility that setting up firm boundaries with her family may result in them reacting negatively at first. This was Karen's first major challenge in taking steps to becoming independent.

Karen worked on breaking the habit of sharing everything with her family. Instead of daily updates with her mother, she met up with her once a week to share news. She refrained from sharing her relationship problems with her father and worked on taking responsibility for her own decision making.

John

John saw that his need for approval had led to him sometimes behaving 'like a doormat'. He also realised that his default setting of either becoming moody and distant or getting aggressive whenever he felt upset was the reason that his relationships so often ended badly. John began to learn the skills of being open and honest about his feelings. He moved from playing the blame game, which was using 'you always' in arguments, to 'I feel', which allowed him to express himself in a non-defensive way.

John saw that he repeated a pattern from his past in his current relationships, and that, in order to break the self-defeating cycle of behaviour, he had focus on valuing his own feelings. He practised saying 'no' to things that he wasn't happy to go along with and started to prioritise what he wanted.

*

As a couple John and Karen agreed on a trial period of living together and working on improving their communication with one another, and setting joint boundaries that protected their relationship.

These steps enabled both John and Karen to invest in their own relationship and be mindful that this was a process that needed time. They were both effectively creating an environment where they could cultivate a healthy functioning relationship.

Self-Help Tips: Asserting Your Boundaries

These very simple steps will ensure that you communicate your feelings assertively, and will set the tone for how you wish to be treated by your partner in return.

1. Stop handing over control to your partner. The first small step to breaking this habit is to express what you'd like to do. Start with the small stuff – for instance, choosing the restaurant or deciding which film to see.

2. Be aware of your body language. Studies suggest that between 55 and 80 per cent of how we communicate is non-verbal.[3] Basic steps like sitting down together, facing your partner and making sure you have their full attention and they have yours is crucial – so turn off all outer distractions like the TV, Xbox, computer or mobile.

3. Body language also includes vocal cues such as voice intonation, rhythm, tone, pitch and style of speaking. So if you want your partner to really listen to you, don't whine or plead but speak slowly and calmly.

4. Take responsibility too. Saying something like, 'I feel taken advantage of sometimes, and I have let this happen too by not speaking up.' Starting a sentence with 'I feel' will ensure that your partner really listens to you and can take on board what you are saying. Starting with 'you always' will leave your partner feeling attacked, and may result in them shutting down, becoming defensive or a row escalating.

TIME TOGETHER, CHORES AND OTHER PRACTICALITIES

When considering boundaries, a key area that needs to be discussed is how much time you as a couple spend together and apart. Couples may have very different ideas about what they mean by time spent together. One person's fantasy of always being together and doing everything as a unit may be another person's idea of hell! Transiting from committed dating to living under one roof brings a change of rhythm to the relationship and the challenge of adjusting to one another. Time spent together before living together may have been wonderful, exciting and fuelled by anticipation. Sex, for instance, may have been fun and spontaneous before, but being under the same roof may bring about a change – one person may expect the spontaneity to continue, while the other may expect sex to settle down to less frequent intervals.

The reality of living together may also impinge on your personal space and routine. Before living together, you may have had time to go to the gym when you wanted, watch what you wanted on telly or spend time down the pub with your friends. Moving in together means thinking about how to maintain your independence without neglecting your partner, feeling stifled or feeling ignored.

Basic everyday tasks also come into sharp focus. While dating, you may have spent weekends at each other's places and not minded one bit about occasionally washing up after dinner. However, when you move in together these practicalities become an everyday event. You may assume that your partner should wash up, and that you will only iron your own clothes. Or you may get fed up because you're doing all the cooking most nights while your partner watches TV.

This may seem as though I am asking you to take the fun and romance out of the relationship! But discussing the practicalities of how you are going to live together is one of the smartest things you as a couple can do in order to save tensions and conflict down the line.

Take a step-by-step approach. For instance, consider the following areas and possible solutions, and then discuss them together. This will help you both to get the conversation started about how you would both like to share time, space and chores, as well as an opportunity to discuss and agree on time apart, family visits and holidays. By being explicit with each other, you'll be able to set practical goals and avoid misunderstandings.

TACKLING THE PRACTICALITIES

The ground rules:

➤ Agree to be fair with each other.

➤ Play to your strengths. If you're better at paying bills promptly, then take on that role. If your partner is more adept at DIY then they can take on that role.

➤ Share undesirables. Take turns to do jobs you may both dislike but that need doing. For instance, cleaning the bathroom.

➤ Ensure balance to avoid resentment. This means making sure neither of you are feeling as though you are doing more than your partner.

Areas To Discuss and Agree On:

Time Together vs Time Apart

➤ Agree how often you would like time to yourself or with your own friends. Perhaps twice a week to the gym, Friday night out with friends.

Holidays
➤ Discuss what the budget is for holidays.
➤ Agree how you would like holidays to be spent. Two weeks together? Or a week together and a week away with friends?

Family Visits
➤ Discuss how much time you would like to spend visiting or having family members visit you.

This will ensure that you are both happy with the frequency and avoid resentments building up.

Self-Help Tips: The Challenges of Moving In

Wanting to live with the one you love most can be a very exciting time, but as illustrated, entering into it without thought, introspection and planning can bring up challenging and unexpected feelings.

Here are seven positive and effective ways to handle the challenges and make this experience a positive and healthy one.

1. When problems occur, it is vital to communicate without blame. While it can be very satisfying to see yourself as the one who is hard done by, and dump all the blame on your partner, it won't get you very far in the long term, all you'll do is maintain a defensive atmosphere. Thinking of your partner as 'the baddy' will intensify negative feelings, which will lead to negative behaviour. Cool down, giving your rational brain a chance to take over from an overly emotional reaction, and then speak.
2. Take the fight out of your voice. Sounding like a ball breaker or a bully will only drive a wedge between you, so

lower your tone, speak slowly, breathe and remember this is someone you care deeply for.

3. Praise, praise, praise. Giving your partner a shopping list of what is wrong with them will just turn them off. Instead, tell them what you love about them and how much you appreciate what they do.

4. Building trust. Yes, jealousy pops up in all relationships from time to time. But letting it eat away at you will become toxic and drive your partner away. Learn to name it, express it, take responsibility for your feelings then move on. If there is a serious trust issue, don't suffer in silence, get help – talk to a counsellor who will try to help you get it into perspective and tackle it in a constructive way.

5. Grow your intimacy. Not everyone wants to be touchy-feely. Some people find it positively toe-curling. However, research shows that positive and loving touch improves well-being, whether it's a newborn or a 90 year old. If you find touch tricky, then start off slow. Hold hands, stroke hair, a shoulder hug, all these touches communicate to your partner that you care about them. The more you build on this the more you'll build closeness and intimacy.

6. Develop your voice. If being single fills you with dread, and in the past you have deferred your own needs in favour of your partner's, breaking the cycle of anxiety is vital. Learning to voice your needs in a partnership is healthy.

7. No one is perfect. Needing your partner to be 'your everything' will be for them hugely unattractive, stifling and eventually will push them away. Taking your partner off the pedestal means that you begin to see them as a real person and not as a romanticised ideal who cannot and must not be faulty in any way.

Living together is a psychological and emotional step as well as a practical one and that's why it is vital to be honest about your expectations, needs and concerns. In fact it is so important that you are open with each other in this way as early as possible. If you can't be honest now, then as time goes on it'll only get harder to speak up. Seize this opportunity to start building a healthy foundation of honest and open communication. It will set the tone for how you constructively handle differences and challenges in future.

PART 2
After Moving In

Chapter 4

Is Long-Term Commitment What I Wanted?

As we've already seen, it is easy to fall in love with someone but it is so much harder to sustain that loving feeling over a long period of time. Life with your partner may sometimes seem like an uphill struggle, and a growing sense of dissatisfaction can turn into 'Is that it? Did I really sign up for this?' Sometimes new feelings can get to you when you're least expecting it and chuck a spanner in the works. Whether it is growing boredom, getting itchy feet or becoming attracted to someone else – all can trigger an emotional upheaval and shift life from a comfortable, predictable rhythm to a messy set of circumstances, destabilising you and causing major upset.

There is absolutely no doubt that relationships have a major influence on our well-being and of course our happiness. When difficulties occur our central concerns become:

➤ Can I make this relationship work again?
➤ Are we headed in the same direction?
➤ Where did the person I fell in love with go?
➤ If I could, would I choose someone different?
➤ Do I really want to be here for the long haul?

In this chapter I am going to focus on how to handle the central question, is a long-term relationship with my partner right for me? I'll use a variety of case studies to illustrate challenging flashpoints. These are here to help you to identify you and your partner's pattern of behaviour that may be causing you to re-evaluate your choices. With self-help tips, you'll be able to recognise what may be going wrong in your own relationship and identify what the underlying problem may be, so that you can learn how to effectively get your relationship from 'back off' to 'back together'.

RELATIONSHIP DISSATISFACTION

As relationships naturally change from lust and passion to becoming more solid, with a few challenges already weathered, some people can start to experience their relationship as a daily grind. So far, you may have had to adjust, readjust and perhaps cope with a number of highs and lows, where you clash and come up against each other's boundaries. Give and take may well have turned into a pattern of predictable assumptions. And once the early excitement of being together wanes, it can seem as though the hard work just begins. There is plenty of research that describes the four-year, seven-year or even nine-year itch.

More than this, life's realities can start to get in the way – from the hard work as well as joy of children, to losing a parent or redundancy, life may well become more physically and emotionally stressful. Sharing difficult feelings with your partner at a tricky time in your relationship can be tough.

Many of us fear the emotions that accompany relationship dissatisfaction. Irritations occur and arguments feel as though they are never very far away, and this mood can feel never-ending, negative and challenging. I often see couples for counselling at this stage, when they've hit a crisis point and the relationship feels very rocky.

It may just be the case of everyday life and demands taking over and as a result you may have stopped communicating properly. Communication is the glue that keeps relationships alive and connected. It's so easy to let this dry up, or become bitter when you're feeling bad, and, of course, all this does is to create greater distance. As a result, being in synchrony with each other may have completely evaporated. Instead of talking honestly and openly, conversations are clipped or defensive. Certainly not the environment for a heart to heart.

There are many deeper relationship issues that can challenge you to wonder whether you really are cut out to be in a long-term relationship with your partner. Just for starters: if sex was the best bit then boredom in the bedroom can trigger negative feelings; roles in a relationship change once children come along and can cause tensions; the pain of an affair can trigger a deeper lack of trust; or if one partner puts career aspirations before home life.

A lot of relationships get stuck here, and some of us may spend a lot of energy trying to restore the feelings that existed right at the start of the relationship. But when you're questioning whether you even want to be in the relationship with your partner, then you know that receiving expensive flowers or a spa weekend away is just not going to be enough to solve it!

Although it might not feel like it now, this phase can actually be a positive and fertile time. There is nothing wrong with re-evaluating a relationship and reflecting on whether it is what you wanted: it's normal to do this as we grow and change and enter different life stages. But it is also incredibly hard when you're knee-deep in a relationship, perhaps feeling hurt and angry or confused, to see clearly what is going on. The key to managing this is to slow down and take a step-by-step approach and tackle how you feel in a constructive and informed way. By following the advice in this chapter, you can navigate your relationship out of trouble and make positive choices about how to handle the difficulties.

RELATIONSHIP SCAFFOLDING

It is crucial to understand exactly what your 'relationship scaffolding' is made up of. By this, I mean you need to examine what your understanding of a long-term relationship should look, feel and behave like.

EXPLORE YOUR RELATIONSHIP SCAFFOLDING

Understanding exactly what a long-term relationship means to you is important, but equally important is working out how strong this belief holds up when problems occur.

Ask yourself:

1. When problems occur in your relationship is your impulse to:
➤ Stay and work it out?
➤ At the first sign of real trouble, run away as fast as possible?
➤ Blame your partner?

2. What kind of emotions come to mind when things go wrong:
➤ Do you feel fearful that the relationship is going to end and you'll be left alone?
➤ Do you feel shame because people will think that you can't sustain a relationship?
➤ Do you feel vulnerable, and hate the thought that you've allowed your partner to get close to you?
➤ What else do you feel?

3. How do you behave when things go wrong:
➤ Do you get angry and blame your partner/your parents/the world?

➤ Do you withdraw and refuse to talk about it?

➤ Do you cry/sulk/walk out?

➤ How else do you behave?

4. What beliefs about relationships come into your mind when problems occur:

➤ Relationships always end badly.

➤ Relationships aren't always smooth sailing and problems have to be worked out.

➤ Relationships are temporary.

➤ Relationships should be perfect; problems mean that my partner is wrong for me.

➤ Good relationships are never challenging.

➤ You can't trust anyone, especially when they get too close to you.

➤ I am unlovable.

➤ I am not meant to be with only one person for the rest of my life.

5. What beliefs from your past do you carry about enduring relationships?

➤ What have your past relationships taught you about love and relationships?

➤ If you've come from a family where divorce features heavily, do you believe that this is inevitable for you?

➤ Did you learn that you should stick at relationships even when they're not working?

➤ Do you come from a family where parents and grandparents were happily together for decades and for you to ditch a long-term relationship would equal failure?

Being really honest with yourself and reflecting on your relationship scaffolding will enable you to gain a clear picture of how your beliefs influence what happens next. Working through these aspects with your partner will also provide you with an excellent set of tools to start communicating constructively and to figure out as a team what both your relationship priorities are.

If your relationship scaffolding reflects back a healthy attitude to your relationship, then that's wonderful. It may simply be the case that poor communication – such as not making time to talk – has led to small niggling problems turning into bigger fights because underlying feelings have not been communicated.

If your relationship scaffolding is reflecting back problems, then it is critical to examine what factors may be getting in the way. Exploring how you communicate, how often you make assumptions about each other and examining what roles you and your partner play out in the relationship will help you to do that in more detail.

COMMUNICATION

So, let's take a closer look at communication. We all know that good communication is key to creating and maintaining a happy and healthy relationship. Communication is more than just talking, it's about how often you make the time to have sex and share that special connection, and it's about non-verbal behaviour: smiling, hugging, holding hands. But when you're right in the middle of angry feelings, sleeves rolled up spoiling for a fight and you don't even know whether you still love your partner or not, then things get a lot trickier.

When you get angry you can find it almost impossible to find the right words to express emotions. When frightened and feeling threatened by what is happening, you may respond by going into 'fight, flight or fright mode'. Classically what happens is that, no matter what the trigger is, a stressed-out and angry couple might:

➤ Fight – start talking or shouting at each other.
➤ Flight – start avoiding one another.
➤ Fright – become so frightened that they don't know what to do.

You might find that your 'default settings' (your habitual, automatic reactions that seem to happen almost without thinking) kick in, so, instead of being honest about your feelings, you might just become avoidant, clingy or even aggressive.

Stress means we stop listening. We continue to shout out our points of view and cannot get past the anger – and anger left to its own devices builds on anger. Dig a little deeper and you'll find that what usually lies underneath the anger is a combination of feelings that reveal that emotional needs are simply not being met.

Poor communication is a common relationship issue. One finding by the Office of National Statistics found that couples spend about 150 minutes a day together – a third of which is spent watching TV, 30 minutes eating and 24 minutes doing housework together. That suggests that proper time spent actively interacting with no distractions is about 6.6 minutes a day! Is it any wonder that there are times when you may think, 'What's the point of sticking with this?'

Let's run with the 6.6-minute daily conversations for a moment. Can you imagine what could be said and shared in this tiny window of time? How rewarding can a relationship be if that's all that is being invested in it? My point is that being in a relationship for the long haul does take effort in order for it to be and feel rewarding.

Falling in love is the passive part of love. For a lot of us, it does 'just happen'. Staying in love is the active part of love.

It takes the effort of both people being present in the process to make it work. If at the first sniff of trouble you are out of the door, then of course you may always find relationships dissatisfying.

MINDREADING AS A FORM OF COMMUNICATION

Mindreading is another form of miscommunication that sometimes occurs when we've been in a relationship for a while. If we have a shared routine, we often falsely believe that we should always be able to sense how our other half is feeling, and they should be able to do the same. Ironically, it is this faulty thinking that reinforces the belief that your partner really doesn't understand you!

Imagine that your partner comes in late from work and slumps in front of the TV, hoping that the kids are in bed and dinner is ready. They might be thinking – 'It's obvious that I'm tired. I just need time to relax and be taken care of.' However, you might be thinking, 'What about me? How dare you treat me like a maid?'

Both points of view are understandable, and if the feelings are spoken as they are meant to be a compromise would be reached. But if the time to talk is missed, honest and open communication is replaced by resentment and irritation.

When this happens, what can come out instead is a stream of defensive anger. This type of defensive conversation is one that I've often heard. One person says, 'Can't you see I'm tired. I'm the one who works all day.' The other responds, 'How dare you? I work too. You don't care about me any more.' Within moments, two people who once thought the world of each other are screaming at each other, unable to see the other's point of view.

COMMUNICATION CHECK-UP

1. How much time do you spend talking to each other in an average week?
2. How much of the conversation is practical – children, bills and such like, and how much is nurturing – sharing how you both feel, hugging and kissing?
3. How many times have you mind read this week?
4. How many times have you rowed this week?
5. When there's a row, do you always have to win, or are you able to concede sometimes?
6. Are you able to pick your battles or is everything up for an argument?

TRAFFIC LIGHT COMMUNICATION

When disagreements become arguments, it can be helpful to think about them in terms of traffic lights. This can help you to quickly assess how best to respond.

➤ **Red.** When you or your partner are seeing red, unquenchable rage is on the menu. There is absolutely no point continuing to try to resolve anything when one of you is in this state. Now is the time to say, 'I need time out to cool down.' If your partner leaves the room because they're the one who is feeling so angry, then don't follow them yelling and screaming, you'll only be adding petrol to the fire. It is vital to give each other some time to calm down.* However, don't leave each other steaming for hours or

---

* Daniel Goleman in his book *Emotional Intelligence*[4] describes beautifully why we need time to cool down. As he says, our primitive brain is full of unfiltered emotions and impulses that kick in first. We need to allow time for the rational brain to catch up so we can respond in an adult state rather than reacting in a more child-like state.

days on end if you can avoid it. Staying angry with one another can lead to self-righteousness and a horrible atmosphere. Remember anger builds on anger. Instead, a break of about an hour should be enough time. Look out for the traffic sign Orange.

➤ **Orange.** This is the time to diffuse it. You are able to be in the same room and to start to look at each other. Body language has softened, from being tense and rigid to softer and more receptive. You are able to get physically closer. Now is the time to speak, in a quieter voice – at this point you can downgrade the anger and give way to a hug.

➤ **Green.** This means you are now ready to talk. You are both more willing to listen to each other. Now is the time to take a deep breath and take it in turns to speak, without interruption. Starting with 'I feel …' and then explaining what upset you, and then allowing your partner to do the same, takes the blame out of the disagreement. It ensures you avoid repeating a negative argument pattern and can move forward.

STEPS TO POSITIVE CONVERSATIONS

It may seem odd, but being honest with your partner about how you really feel can be one of the hardest things to do. Okay, so your partner may have witnessed the vaginal birth of your three kids, but sharing that you sometimes feel unattractive and worry that he may not fancy you any more can feel embarrassing. Why? Because no one likes to feel that vulnerable. What if he agrees? What if he says something you won't like? All these fears may prevent honest communication and lead to defensive outbursts instead – shouting, screaming, crying, sulking … The truth is your partner may be feeling vulnerable too. Making a pact to be honest with each other is the first step to crisis survival.

Changing behaviour takes practice and motivation on both sides. However, there are effective techniques that can help break the row cycle and make conversations calmer, more honest and more fulfilling.

The more regularly you both practise positive ways to communicate, the more these behaviours will become part of the natural rhythm of your relationship.

Self-Help Tips: Better Communication

1. Create a specific and special time to talk – put it on the calendar or in your diary.
2. Break the tension by changing the scenery and going for a walk together. Studies have shown the numerous physical- and mental-health benefits of walking. It can help improve mood and decrease tension.[5]
3. Learn to listen and give each other proper attention.
4. Take it in turns to listen and then speak. Don't blame, be responsible. Starting a sentence off with 'I feel …' is more desirable and creates a safer environment for honesty, and will mean your partner listens, instead of the accusatory, 'You always …'.
5. Learn to pick your battles. If you fight over every tiny little thing then your relationship becomes a seething battleground of defensive behaviour. Learning to let go of the small, insignificant stuff means that when there *is* something important to say it is heard and received rather than met with, 'Here we go again!'

These ground rules lay the foundation for a more resilient partnership by creating the safe space to express your individual needs, release negative emotions safely and strengthen your bond with one another. The bonus also is that it means rows are diffused quickly.

Sometimes just being able to pinpoint where negative or challenging feelings are coming from can be a huge relief, and allow you to take these positive steps to resolving problems and getting your relationship back on track. However, sometimes, deep-seated problems can be very challenging and deeply affect our ability to stay for the long haul.

COMMON PITFALLS

There are common relationship problems that we may all experience from time to time. For instance, it is perfectly normal when you have been together for a while to fall into relationship bad habits. For instance, expecting that your partner will have a cup of tea ready for you the moment you walk in from work every evening. This may be based on the fact that your partner has almost always done this for you, and so you've stopped acknowledging this generous gesture and simply forgotten to thank them. Over time, your partner may start to feel resentful and taken for granted, and one day just stops doing it.

Because it is so easy to fall into patterns of assumed roles, or allow communication with each other to become low priority, or simply get into the habit of believing that your partner should by now be able to know what you're thinking just by looking at you; it is vital to be vigilant. Allowing relationships to slide into bad habits could store up far worse problems if issues aren't confronted and dealt with early.

ASSUMED ROLES

Settling into a relationship sometimes means that both parties assume particular roles. You may have a long-held belief that it is the man's role to be the provider and financial carer, whereas it is the woman's role to take care of hearth and home. This is absolutely fine, as long as you're both agreed to it. Not discussing basic differences of opinion like this, however, can be catastrophic and cause unnecessary resentments. You may truly believe that you're with someone who takes you for granted and treats you like a maid. Your partner may see you as undermining and unsupportive. Not talking about what your beliefs actually are leads to entrenched positions. It also means that if circumstances change both parties find it even more difficult to stay the distance.

MAKING ASSUMPTIONS

1. How many assumptions have you made this week about whose turn it is to do something?
2. When your partner behaves in a manner that you feel is inconsiderate (e.g. makes themselves a cup of tea in the morning, but doesn't make you one), what is your first thought about them?
3. What role in the relationship have you assumed (e.g. carer, healer or problem solver)?
4. What role have you cast your partner in (e.g. protector, provider or listener)?
5. Have these roles made it difficult for you to see each other differently?

Self-Help Tips: Creating Equilibrium
In the early days of love, being kind and thoughtful to each other seemed so easy. As time goes on and the intensity abates, it becomes easier to put less effort in – after all you're under one roof now!

Making sure give and take is fair in your relationship is crucial to ensuring you maintain your dynamic equilibrium. Here's how:

1. If you're forgetful and your partner finds this annoying because they almost always have to sort things out for you – get organised and get a calendar!

2. If you do too much for your partner, and this makes you feel resentful, learn to step back and let them step up.
3. If your partner likes to sit down and discuss things endlessly, and you prefer not to, then create a specific finite amount of time to do so as a compromise.

RECYCLING THE PAST

It is quite common for people to recycle unresolved feelings from the past into their present-day relationships, as already discussed in Chapter 1 (see pages 35–8). This happens because people bring to the table the emotional imprint of significant others who have influenced them, as well as internalised beliefs about themselves in relation to others and the world in general. It is not uncommon to see unresolved wounds from the past played out in present-day relationships, and sometimes couples can get stuck in this dynamic.

Imagine a wife whose husband's behaviour reminds her so much of her 'useless' father, who – without realising it – treats her husband with the rage that she felt for her father.

Becoming consciously aware of this process is crucial to breaking this cycle and beginning to work through any problems.

———

Case Study: Three's a Crowd

Max (45) and Jasmine (39) had been living together for 12 years. They made the decision very early on that marriage wasn't for them and they were very happy cohabiting. They'd always wanted a big family and felt that for them living together and having children was a more important symbol of commitment and togetherness. They had seven happy years together and spent much time together talking, sharing and looking forward to starting a family.

When Jasmine got pregnant, they were both very excited and Max started enthusiastically decorating the nursery. However, as the

pregnancy progressed, Max started to become a little more distant.
He seemed more distracted and short-tempered, which was unusual
behaviour. Jasmine asked him if everything was okay.

He put it down to work stress and for a while things went back
to normal. But once the baby was born, Max's behaviour got worse.
He would come home late from work and leave very early in the
morning. At weekends he didn't want to be around the home and
went off to the pub with his friends.

Jasmine was devastated. She couldn't understand what was
happening and his lack of support resulted in her getting depressed.
It was around this time that a mutual friend told her that Max had
been seen getting very close to another woman at the pub.

She confronted him, and Max admitted that although he wasn't
having an affair, this woman paid him more attention than she did,
and that since the baby was born she'd been ignoring his needs.
Jasmine felt incredibly hurt and angry and demanded that he moved
out. After much persuasion from her mother, Jasmine allowed him
back into the family home and things settled back into some kind of
unhappy routine.

Crunch Time
When Jasmine got pregnant with their second child a few years later,
the same thing happened again. Max became close to a woman
from work and confided his feelings to her. Jasmine couldn't believe
it. The relationship was in crisis and Jasmine decided she wanted to
end it. Max begged her not to, and they decided to enter counselling
for the sake of the children. Through counselling it became evident
what the key issues were.

Max
With counselling Max explored his psychological history. He described
coming from a very happy family upbringing, and as an only child
was the centre of his parents' world, until they had decided to
become foster carers when he was 11. Each time a new child came
into the family home he felt as though he was effectively pushed

out. Although his parents had talked to him openly and honestly about the rewards and challenges they may all face as a family, he had felt real ambivalence. On the one hand he felt excited at the thought of having someone else to play with, and on the other hand he felt jealous and abandoned. He played up at school and went from being known as a very well-behaved and friendly boy, to being labelled as angry and aggressive. Although his parents worked very hard to resolve these issues, Max struggled to come to terms with the emotional disruptions at home.

Max began to recognise that he treated his children as a threat to his happiness with Jasmine. He felt so much guilt about hurting Jasmine, yet at the same time wanted to hurt her to get back at her for 'abandoning' him. He was effectively carrying his residual rage from his childhood and transferring his fears on to Jasmine and their children.

Jasmine

Jasmine described her childhood as an emotional roller coaster. She was brought up by her mother after her father had died, after a short illness, when she was seven. Although her mother had been very loving she had relied heavily on Jasmine emotionally. Jasmine hadn't really felt supported with her own grieving process and all attention had been given to her mother. Jasmine had to grow up fast and take on more responsibility. When her mother got remarried and had another baby when Jasmine was 13, she became mini-mum to her little sister – and willingly did everything for her. She became the emotional carer in the family, but often also felt that she was on the fringes of the newly recreated nuclear family.

Jasmine recognised that her emotional needs often went unmet, and she'd learnt to prioritise the feelings of others before her own. This was the role that she'd been cast in from a very young age and continued to take on as an adult: whether it was with Max, family or friends. She realised that she had accommodated many of Max's needs throughout the relationship, without clearly expressing what she wanted. She'd gone along with not getting married, even though it was something she longed for because to her it meant *security. Things had been fine up until she got pregnant because Max had been her only priority.*

She recognised that she hadn't dealt with the devastation of his first emotional affair because she just couldn't face the thought of losing him. Although she knew deep down that they needed help as a couple, she had wanted to believe that having another child would stop Max from ever leaving her.

Jasmine began to see that her coping mechanism from her past had been denial. Growing up in an environment where she didn't feel able to express her own needs had resulted in her denying her own feelings and intuitions in order to fit in with others. She realised that she often felt the incongruence between how she felt deep down and how she actually behaved. She would feel angry and yet behave as though she was perfectly happy.

Jasmine and Max recognised that trust had been severely damaged and that this would take a long time to repair.

The Way Forward

Through counselling Max and Jasmine focused first of all on whether they were both willing to recommit to building trust again. Jasmine took steps to dismantle denial as her default setting in order to cope with stress whenever she saw problems ahead. Max challenged the script of his past that had led to his deep-seated feelings of abandonment. Over time, and with commitment and a lot of patience on both sides, Max and Jasmine began to slowly rebuild trust and honesty in their relationship.

———

AFFAIRS: DEAL-BREAKER OR DEAL MAKER?

The unpalatable fact is that affairs do happen. Statistics show that roughly 30 to 40 per cent of people in a marriage or long-term relationship have been unfaithful.

First of all I believe it is vital to work out what your relationship boundaries are. You may enter a relationship making the assumption that you both have a similar understanding of what constitutes an affair until something happens that throws this assumption out of the window. Or you may believe that you have strong-held beliefs that affairs are bad and that you'd never entertain such a notion, until something happens to destabilise you.

HOW WOULD YOU DEFINE BEING UNFAITHFUL?

Ask yourself these questions and then ask your partner to do the same. This enables you both to understand the boundaries that your relationship operates within and your tolerance levels *before* either of you transgress beyond those boundaries.

➤ Openly sexually flirting with someone else other than your partner.
➤ Texting flirtatious messages to someone else.
➤ Sexting (exchanging sexually explicit texts) with someone else.
➤ Confiding your deepest feelings to someone other than your partner.
➤ Kissing someone else.
➤ Having sex with someone else.

If your tolerance levels are vastly different then this *is* something that you need to work on right now. If you don't think that there's anything wrong with flirting at a party, but your partner expresses that they'd find this intolerable, then you both need to work this through.

If you are the flirt, ask yourself:

➤ Are you flirting because you need the attention of others?

> ➤ Do you think it's just part of your nature – you have always flirted with everybody and your partner knew this from the start?
> ➤ Do you enjoy making your partner jealous?
> ➤ Is your flirting filled with sexual intent? I.e. do you hope or expect something more to develop?
>
> If it is you that hates to see your partner flirting, ask yourself:
>
> ➤ Do you hate your partner flirting because it makes you feel insecure?
> ➤ Are you not sure if you trust them not to overstep the mark?
> ➤ Do you feel that your partner is committed to *you*, so flirting is simply out of the question?
>
> Ask yourself the last two sets of questions for sexting, kissing and confiding feelings too. Tackling your individual and joint understanding of social behaviour will help you identify what you both will and will not tolerate.

For some, an affair is a deal-breaker and the relationship comes to an abrupt end. A person may have chosen to have an affair as a way of ending their relationship and therefore there is no way back. For others an affair causes such unbearable pain that they simply cannot tolerate the relationship any more. But an affair can just be a red-flag symptom of a more deep-seated problem.

Denial may have played its part in destabilising a relationship. Your partner may have been trying to communicate unhappiness in the relationship, but you may have found it easier to ignore the problems.

ARE YOU IN DENIAL?

If you have a tendency to bury your head in the sand (even when you suspect that your partner may be having an affair) and are in the habit of denying deeper problems, then exploring what is going on for you may be the key to uncovering and dealing with your deep-seated fears. Ask yourself:

➤ What is it I am so afraid of when it comes to confronting difficult feelings?
➤ What will happen if I don't face up to my fears?
➤ Could I cope with suspicious feelings and turning a blind eye for years to come?
➤ Is that better than facing life on my own?

If denial is your coping strategy then keeping a journal of your feelings could help you to confront your feelings and bring them into sharp focus. Sometimes working through these feelings in a safe space with a counsellor can also really help to tackle deeper issues.

IS YOUR AFFAIR A DISTRESS SIGNAL?

If you suspect having an affair is your way of communicating distress, then ask yourself:

➤ Is having an affair my way of getting emotional or sexual gratification?
➤ Is it my way of boosting my self-esteem?
➤ Have I thought about the effects it will have on my partner and the ripple effect on family, friends and work colleagues?

> ➤ Have I thought about the consequences an affair would have on my child/children?
> ➤ Is this my way out of an unhappy relationship?

Self-Help Tips: the Building Blocks of Trust

Once trust has been damaged then, make no mistake, there is a long and very challenging road ahead for both of you. There are seven key steps to mending the broken fences of trust if you are *both* willing to reinvest.

1. If it is you that had the affair, then take responsibility for your actions. Blaming your partner will get you nowhere.
2. If your partner had the affair, deciding to forgive them is your first step.
3. Make a pact of honesty and commit to it. It's vital not to keep secrets from each other as this would be toxic to rebuilding trust.
4. Consistently reassure your partner if they need it – they deserve your empathy.
5. Regularly check in with each other. This could mean spending time reconnecting with one another at the end of each day.
6. Respect that your partner is deeply hurt and it may take time for them to want hugs, kisses or sex. Take it slowly.
7. Get help. Talking to a professional therapist in a non-judgemental setting can give you both the space and the tools to work through difficult feelings.

TOXIC RELATIONSHIPS

Sometimes, no matter how hard you try, it is best for a relationship to end. If you find yourself in a situation where you are afraid, threatened, harmed, isolated from the outside world or feeling controlled, then you may be in a very toxic environment and need to get help.

Recognising that your partner is controlling is a critical first step. Early on in the relationship, your partner may come across as very charming, self-assured and charismatic. They may flatter you by their undivided attention or by their feelings of jealousy if another person pays you a compliment. This can be very seductive.

It can be difficult when you're in the middle of a relationship, trying to make things work, to pay attention to nagging fears and doubts – the tendency can be to bury your head in the sand and carry on. This is an unhelpful strategy, which will eventually catch up with you.

IS YOUR RELATIONSHIP TOXIC?
Ask yourself:

➤ How does my partner make me feel when we are together?
➤ How much does my partner praise me or put me down?
➤ Does my partner behave charmingly in front of other people and dreadfully behind closed doors?
➤ Do I like my partner most of the time/some of the time/hardly at all?
➤ How have my feelings about my partner changed over time?

Keep a Diary of Incidents
If your partner has behaved badly towards you note in your journal:

➤ How it makes you feel.

➤ How you respond to it.
➤ What happens afterwards.

Ask yourself:

➤ What is it about this relationship that you need?
➤ What keeps you from leaving?
➤ Are you benefiting in some way from staying in the relationship?

Are you staying in the relationship because:

➤ You believe you can change your partner for the better?
➤ You make a positive difference to their life?
➤ They've told you that they are nothing without you?
➤ They've threatened to hurt themselves if you leave?

Case Study: Enough is Enough

Bob (60) and Lizzy (56) had been married for 30 years. They had three children who all lived independently now. They'd met through a political group that they both belonged to. The night they met, Bob was giving a heart-felt speech at a local conference and Lizzy found him both charismatic and passionate. He was instantly drawn to her beauty and positive energy.

Although they came from different cultural and religious backgrounds, they found that they had a lot in common. They had shared political beliefs and wanted similar things from life.

Within a year of meeting, they were married and had their first son. Bob was a deputy head at the local secondary school and was driven to be headmaster by the time he was 35. Lizzy and Bob had agreed that when the children came along, Lizzy would drop down to working a couple of days a week so that the children could have at least one parent around most of the time.

To the outside world, Lizzy and Bob were the perfect family. Their three sons were bright, friendly and outgoing, and as a couple, they socialised together a lot, had numerous dinner parties and were often seen at various fundraisers and charity events. But there was more going on beneath the surface.

Lizzy

Lizzy was one of four children, and was brought up in what she described as a traditional Italian Catholic family. Her parents had moved to the UK just after she was born. Her father ran his own business and her mother stayed at home to raise the children. Lizzy's father was the head of the family, and everything ran like clockwork, because he demanded it. Her parents never rowed and she perceived their marriage as a secure one. As the youngest, Lizzy was shielded from problems by her three older brothers. She sometimes sensed that her mother was unhappy, but being 'daddy's little girl', and getting so much positive attention from him, she dismissed these feelings.

It was only when she was older and married herself, that Lizzy's brothers opened up about their childhood. She discovered that her brothers resented their father and experienced him as a bully. Although her mother never really complained she was desperately unhappy, but never felt able to do anything about it. She kept her feelings to herself to her dying day.

Lizzy's brothers weren't particularly fond of Bob when they first met him. They found him to be arrogant and pushy. One brother in particular, Phil, who Lizzy was closest to, expressed his worries to her. Lizzy dismissed his concerns, saying that Bob was a wonderful man.

Once married, her brothers visited her less and less. They couldn't tolerate Bob's behaviour; witnessing how he often just needled Lizzy and picked faults in her. When the children came along, Bob's behaviour calmed down. He was an attentive father, who valued education and wanted his sons to do well.

Bob

Bob moved to Britain from India when he was ten, with his aunt and uncle, in order to take up a scholarship at school. He was extremely bright and had worked hard to earn his place at a top private school.

Bob described his experience of growing up as one of feeling like an outsider. He was the youngest of five, and was the smallest and the darkest. He was picked on a lot at primary school in India for being so small and dark, and even his family mocked him, saying he was the black sheep. He wasn't close to his parents and they encouraged him to take up the scholarship and seek opportunities elsewhere.

When he moved to England he felt emancipated. He had the perfect opportunity to reinvent himself and shake off a growing sense of inferiority. He did well at school and later excelled at university. He'd found a way to feel special using his intellect. This, however, masked an underlying lack of confidence and low self-esteem. He often overcompensated for these feelings by becoming dominant in arguments, arrogant and bullish. In relationships with women he was attentive and loving up until the point at which they disagreed with him: then he would become angry and aggressive. He often felt that he needed to control those around him in order to feel good enough.

Crunch Time

As a family unit, each member had become adept at creating a positive image of themselves to the outside world. Lizzy had taught the boys how to manage their father's moods and placate him. Although Bob was a good father, his parenting came with conditions. The boys had to be outstanding academically. He treated them as though they were an extension of himself. When they did well, he felt he'd succeeded. If they didn't excel at something, he felt that they'd failed him. This became an intolerable situation as the boys got older. Although Lizzy tried to smooth things over, her sons challenged her and got angry with her for supporting Bob when he was being totally unreasonable. Lizzy could see how unhappy her sons were becoming and during their teens the whole family entered family counselling.

Bob tried to dominate the therapy sessions and blamed Lizzy for their sons' bad behaviour and lack of respect towards him. He accused Lizzy for failing in her duties as his wife. After every counselling session, Bob accused the therapist of taking Lizzy's side over his, and eventually stopped attending – stating that it was a waste of time.

It was during this time that Lizzy first thought about leaving Bob. He had started physically pushing her – not quite hitting her but enough for her to feel threatened. She felt very alone but too ashamed to tell anyone what was going on. She worried about how she would support her sons if she left. She decided that she would stay with Bob until the boys had left home in order to offer them the security and structure of a home life.

Lizzy became more and more withdrawn after all three boys had left home. She felt that she no longer had the strength to leave and often felt very isolated. She didn't want to tell anyone how unhappy she was.

Her best friend, who had often dropped hints that she knew all was not well, decided to directly confront her. She noticed that Lizzy had lost a drastic amount of weight and was deeply concerned. It was with her friend's help that Lizzy secretly planned her exit. She contacted her brother and, bit by bit, started to move small possessions out of the house. One evening when Bob was at an open evening Lizzy finally left him.

The Way Forward

It had taken an enormous amount of courage for Lizzy to leave. She moved in with her brother and his wife who offered her much-needed support. Lizzy's sister-in-law worked as a therapist and suggested that she enter counselling just to help get her feelings in perspective.

It was during these counselling sessions that Lizzy began to question why she had stayed in such a toxic environment for so long. She had truly believed that creating a loving home for her sons was best with two parents, but she started to see how although she'd tried to shield them, her sons had been negatively affected.

Lizzy recognised how her own upbringing had offered her a template for relationships. She experienced her father as the backbone of the family and her mother in the supporting role. Although her brothers had had a more negative experience of their father, he had always treated Lizzy differently. To him, she was special and needed taking care of. He had only ever got angry with her once, when she wanted to go away for a weekend with some friends and he'd put his foot down. Lizzy realised how in some ways, she'd married her father – a loving yet controlling man, who feared losing those he loved.

Lizzy talked to her sons about how they felt and was shocked to discover that they'd wanted their parents to split up years ago. They felt very loyal to their mother because they saw their father as emotionally controlling and inflexible.

Bob was in a state of shock at Lizzy's sudden departure. He was confused because he simply couldn't understand what had gone wrong. He pleaded with his sons to tell him where she'd gone. Bob went through a painful cycle of emotions. He blamed her for everything going wrong, then he blamed his children for not taking his side, then he blamed his family for treating him so badly growing up.

Bob found it difficult to look at himself and see what his role was in the break-up of his marriage. Lizzy leaving him brought up buried feelings of inadequacy, and he re-experienced feeling like an outsider.

It took six months for Lizzy to finally speak to Bob on the phone. When they'd finalised their divorce Lizzy encouraged Bob to get help. His anger was pushing his sons away. Feeling isolated from his family, Bob finally decided to attend a domestic violence programme, where he started to change his ways.

Self-Help Tips: Self-Preservation for Toxic Relationships

Being in a toxic relationship can be an incredibly lonely experience. You may want to reach out and get support, but feel too afraid or even embarrassed to do so. These important steps will help guide you as to how to handle the emotional and practical challenges.

1. Surround yourself with healthy friends (i.e. those who are sympathetic and caring). Keep your support system around you – don't be tempted to cut people out of your life in order to please your partner.
2. Be aware of who you confide in. If your friends criticise you, it might be because they too are stuck in an unhappy situation, fearful to change, and they want to keep you stranded with them.
3. Sometimes it can feel impossible to think clearly while in the middle of emotional turbulence and doubt. This is the time to talk to a professional counsellor or therapist who can help you in a non-judgemental and supportive environment.
4. If your relationship is causing you more harm than good and, no matter what you do, things aren't really changing for the better, then getting support for yourself and taking decisive steps to protect your well-being when you're ready to leave is crucial.

WORKING THROUGH RELATIONSHIP CHALLENGES

It is completely normal to expect some challenges to emerge along the way, when sharing your life long term with someone else – this is part of the relationship journey. There may be some issues that are clear to see from the get-go, and others that pop up as life settles into its own rhythm. When things go wrong and upset the relationship balance the important point to remember is that you do have the ability to choose how you handle and respond to the challenges. When both of you put in the effort to be honest and open about what is going on, you can then take positive steps to move forward constructively and successfully handle any of the problems together.

Chapter 5
Tying the Knot

A marriage or commitment proposal can spark feelings of excitement, nervousness, anxiety, hope and wish fulfilment in us, and has the potential to send our nearest and dearest into a positively giddy state. Even the language used about the journey to getting married or having a civil partnership is weighted with expectation. We want to hear all about *the* proposal, we want to see *the* engagement ring, we can't wait for *the* big day and are dying to see *the* dress.

The wedding industry, according to research, is big business and some people spend tens of thousands of pounds wanting to ensure that their wedding day is a day to remember.

The 'Disneyfication' of the big day may sometimes feel as though it is overshadowing just what getting married is all about – it may lead some of us to believe that the wedding day is the final destination of a relationship, rather than part of the on-going relationship journey. It is not surprising that people may lose focus on the importance of what marriage actually means.

We may not always think through in detail what's driving our feelings about getting married, or discuss with our partner how they honestly feel about it. We may get so swept up in the excitement and enthusiasm from those around us, that we lose perspective on why we may want to get married in the first place. Or it may be marriage number two, three or four, filled with hope and promises to yourself to do things differently this time round. That's why it is so important to slow down and take a step-by-step look at what's behind your decision to spend the rest of your life with this person.

This step is imbued with a complexity of emotions and multiple influences like personal expectations, past experiences, upbringing, hopes and dreams, and possibly pressure from family and friends to settle down. And all these factors play their part in informing the decision about whether to get married or not.

In this chapter, I'm primarily going to focus on the significance of what your big day means to you, what your expectations and hopes are, what is influencing your decision to get married and how you and your partner can handle this exciting yet challenging occasion together.

This is important to do whether it is your first time getting married or not. The process of *maintaining* a long-term commitment forms a crucial part of this, as is discussed in depth in the previous chapter.

The first step is to examine what your thoughts, feelings and expectations are about marriage.

THE GETTING MARRIED QUIZ

It is important to do the quiz together with your partner. This is a fantastic opportunity for you both to sit down, take a deep breath and openly discuss your feelings, hopes and expectations. Being on the same page is so crucial and it's vital that neither of you feel pressurised to get married.

My reasons for wanting to get married are (choose as many statements as you like and add your own):

➤ I want to spend the rest of my life with my partner.
➤ I am deeply in love.
➤ We have a great companionship.
➤ I want to declare to the world that we are a couple.
➤ We can have sex.
➤ We can pool our financial resources.
➤ We can save money.
➤ It is an important part of my culture.
➤ We can have children.

My expectations for marriage are:
➤ I will feel more secure.
➤ My partner and I will be able to do more together.
➤ I will have someone to take care of.
➤ I will have someone to take care of me.

I believe that marriage means:
➤ We are exclusive to each other.
➤ We live together, but have an open marriage.
➤ We will stay together in sickness and in health.
➤ We will have our fairy-tale ending.

Marriage is the next logical step for me because:
➤ We live together anyway.
➤ We have kids together.
➤ The kids want us to get married.
➤ Our first child is on the way.
➤ We want to have kids within a marriage.
➤ All my friends are getting married.

My hopes for marriage are:
➤ Getting married will keep us together.
➤ Being married will stop my partner straying.

➤ Being married will stop me straying.
➤ We will be committed to each other.
➤ I've dreamed of a fabulous wedding day since I was little.
➤ I learnt a lot from my first marriage and I have a second chance to get it right.

I need my partner to make an official commitment to me because:
➤ I don't like being alone.
➤ I worry that no one else will want me.
➤ Both our families expect us to get married.
➤ I want to celebrate what we have with my friends and family.
➤ I want to start a family and this will make it secure.

Marriage means:
➤ Permanency.
➤ Forever.
➤ Unbreakable bond.
➤ For life.
➤ For now.
➤ Temporary.
➤ Loss of freedom.
➤ Loss of independence.

Doing this quiz together will help you and your partner to be honest with each other about what you both want. If you find that your motives for marriage are vastly different, then you need to think very seriously about your next step.

Notice red-flag areas (these are points of fundamental difference) that reflect where you may be pulling in very different directions. So, for instance, you want to get married in order to have a child, but your partner believes that you don't need to tie the knot in order to start a family. It is important that you don't ignore doubts or areas of concern in the hope that marriage will magically make problems disappear – because sadly it won't. In fact, studies clearly show that it's more likely that existing problems will be amplified. It is therefore important to make the right decision for yourself, with your eyes open.

HOW YOU FEEL ABOUT GETTING MARRIED

If you have any serious doubts, then do this exercise to explore how you feel now and how you may feel in the future if you go ahead and get married.

Okay, take a deep breath and be honest ... and ask yourself:

➤ What similar feelings do we share about marriage?
➤ Where do we differ?
➤ Are we able to compromise and meet in the middle?
➤ How do I think our different motives for getting married will affect us:
  1. One year into marriage,
  2. Five years into marriage,
  3. Ten years into marriage?
➤ How do we deal with challenges at the moment?
➤ Am I hoping that things will get better over time?
➤ How will I handle the relationship if things don't improve after marriage?

These questions will help you assess for yourself whether marriage is the best next step for you or not.

If you find that you're both in agreement about your reasons for getting married, and feel happy to proceed, then that's fantastic. However, there are common areas that some couples do encounter, that can cause problems and that need to be properly handled before taking the next step. These areas include those about the wedding day itself and the marriage that follows. Don't dismiss the wedding day concerns out of hand, as they can often be a sign of deeper problems.

SLIDING INTO MARRIAGE

There are couples who have been together for a number of years, and started a family, who may effectively slide into marriage. So much of their lives may already be entwined, from paying the bills to raising a family. However, for one person, marriage may be the next logical step towards a full and legal commitment, while the other may feel marriage is unnecessary and not want to feel tied down. This can cause major problems.

——————

Case Study: Just Marry Me

Elaine (29) and Theo (36) had been living together for five years. When Elaine met Theo, she said that she knew straight away that this was the man she wanted to marry and have a family with. Theo had spent a few years living on his own and had always maintained that he enjoyed his own company. But meeting Elaine changed everything and he felt that he'd finally met his equal and his soul mate. Elaine had always wanted to get married and emulate the loving relationship that her parents had with one another. Theo was happy for the two of them to just live together.

So, when Elaine proposed to Theo two years into their relationship, he turned her down, stating that their relationship was perfect as it was. She was deeply hurt by this rejection, but kept these feelings to herself and hoped that, over time, he'd come around to the idea of marriage.

But whenever the subject of marriage came up, or they were invited to a friend's wedding, Theo would feel the urge to flee. He was often teased by their mutual friends about his attitudes to marriage, and he would always explain that his parents had a happy and loving bond without the need for a piece of paper to validate their relationship, and that's how he wanted things to be for himself and Elaine.

Elaine

Elaine came from a very close-knit family. She was the youngest of four daughters and all her siblings were married with families of their own. Her parents had been married for 37 years, and she saw their relationship as the perfect model for marriage. Her sisters' weddings were big events in the family calendar and no expense was spared to ensure that the big day for each of them was beautiful. Elaine's family were looking forward to organising her special day and often expressed that she'd make a gorgeous bride. Elaine wanted what her other family members had, which was the security of a legal commitment within a loving relationship.

Theo

Theo was brought up with two older brothers. His parents had been together for 40 years but weren't married. His parents were very clear from the outset that marriage wasn't for them and that what was more important to them was to be faithful, loyal and committed to each other. Theo's eldest brother was married, the middle one wasn't. Theo's relationship with his family was cordial, they saw each other at Christmas time, for birthdays and other family events. They weren't a particularly demonstrative family, but would offer support if needed. Theo grew up with these messages around him and cultivated his own beliefs, which were that being committed to one person didn't need legal validation.

Crunch Time

When Elaine became pregnant, four years into their relationship, she tackled Theo again about marriage. She wanted to have a child within a legal context and felt that this was important to her and to their unborn child. This caused a huge disagreement between them, as Theo felt that they were already in a committed and loving relationship, and expressed disappointment that she didn't feel that him being loyal and committed to her was good enough.

The reality of Elaine's pregnancy and mounting pressure from friends and family to do the right thing caused Theo to rethink his position. Elaine's parents often asked them when they were getting married and expressed concern that their grandchild would be born out of wedlock.

Finally, Theo agreed, and felt that maybe this was best for their child in the long run. They got married when Elaine was six months pregnant. It was a small celebration, with close family and friends. Elaine described it as one of the happiest days of her life and finally felt secure. She now felt that at last her perfect family picture was complete.

Theo, on the other hand, became increasingly dissatisfied, and this became more pronounced once their son was born. He complained of feeling stifled and showed signs of anxiety.

The Way Forward

The added pressures of becoming parents now meant that Elaine and Theo had little quality time to sit down and talk to each other properly. They both decided that they needed extra support and agreed to have some counselling.

As the sessions progressed, their core differences became very clear. For Elaine, marriage meant security and a full commitment. She also admitted that she often worried that without marriage, Theo would find it easier to end their relationship. She'd felt but never discussed these insecurities with him.

Theo thought marriage was unnecessary and felt resentful that Elaine needed a piece of paper in order to make her feel more secure. He felt as though she didn't fully trust him, and this made him feel angry.

It was clear that these issues from their relationship hadn't been addressed and, as time went on, had simply got buried in the routine of everyday life. But the process of getting married had acted as a catalyst for difficult feelings to resurface, and the birth of their son had brought these differences into even sharper focus.

Elaine opened up about how she'd often experienced Theo as emotionally distant. She described how he wouldn't cuddle her as often as she would have liked. She felt that he preferred to socialise without her and that he actively encouraged her to spend more time with her own friends. She admitted that she sometimes felt as though she was in a part-time relationship. But she'd been too afraid to openly challenge him about how he sometimes made her feel. Instead, she had hoped that a marriage commitment would bring them closer.

Theo described how he'd fallen in love with Elaine because of her independent spirit, which he felt faded away as the relationship went on. He felt irritated by her constant need to get married and hoped that, over time, she'd get the message that he didn't want to go down that route. He admitted that her getting pregnant was the main reason he decided to stay in the relationship and agree to marriage.

Having a baby within this context caused a lot of strain between the two of them and they struggled to make the relationship work. Sadly, a year later, they made the painful decision to separate.

———

You may be in a relationship that has been established for some time that has underlying issues that remain unresolved. You may have ignored warning behaviours in the past and found creative ways to explain and justify them to yourself. There may be alarm bells from friends and family warning you that the relationship isn't right. However, you may strongly believe that with the security of marriage, things will improve and change for the better. Wishful thinking like this can lead you to be blind to the full details of what is really going on in your relationship.

Self-Help Tips: Listening Out for Differences

1. Start by examining your relationship properly. Draw up a list of what is good about it and what is worrying you.
2. Pay attention to the detail in your relationship. What happens when you ask your partner about getting married? Notice whether they answer you openly and honestly, or avoid the subject all together. Notice how you handle the response.
3. Notice whether you are truly listening to your partner's responses or interpreting them to hear what you want to hear. An excellent way to tune in to yourself is to pick up on your physical responses to what your partner is saying. For example:

➤ Do you feel as though your heart is sinking?
➤ Does your heart rate increase?
➤ Do you tense up? What other physical sensations do you experience?

These physical sensations are telling you how you honestly feel, so don't ignore them.

1. Pay attention to what family and friends are saying about it.
2. Enlist the support of close friends whom you trust. Difficult I know, but ask them to be honest with you.
3. If you feel that you need extra support, then seeing a counsellor to work through your doubts is a great way forward.

It is vital to pay attention to how you are feeling, so that you don't end up in a relationship that makes you unhappy.

Having the courage to walk away from a situation that is not good for you will leave room to have a relationship that is great for you.

THE GIDDY WEDDING

Sometimes people meet, fall head over heels in love and decide very quickly to get married. This can be a highly intoxicating and exciting time. Both people can feel carried away on a sea of emotional bliss and imagine a wonderful future life together. They may even run off to Las Vegas to tie the knot. Now I'm not saying that you can't meet and fall in love with someone, marry them three weeks later and live together happily for the next 50 years! But these cases are the exception rather than the rule.

What comes next is where the hard work begins. Once you've shaken the confetti out of your hair and wiped the wedding cake crumbs off your partner's lips, you may wake up a few months later and wonder who on earth the stranger is lying next to you in bed!

It is crucial to explore your motives for wanting to get married quickly. These may include having the opportunity to have the dream wedding that you've always wanted, feeling pressurised by family to settle down quickly, even rebelling against family advice to wait before tying the knot. Whatever the reason, giving yourself a chance to think clearly before pushing ahead can save you heartache further down the line.

———

Case Study: I Love You – Let's Get Married!

Justine (23) and Phil (31) met while on a two-week holiday in Italy. Justine was there with her three girlfriends, and Phil was there with two of his brothers. They happened to be staying at the same resort, and within a couple of days were inseparable. They talked and shared a lot with each other very quickly. Phil had been in the army for nine years, serving abroad, and had just over eight months left to complete his tour of duty. He had a couple of months' leave before he had to return back to service. Justine shared that she was getting over a broken heart because her ex-boyfriend had broken off their engagement a few months earlier. Her friends had decided that she needed to get away and have some fun.

When they returned home, she and Phil continued their relationship and had six precious weeks together before he returned to work. In that time, they became really close. They met each other's families and friends, and Justine admitted to her best friend that she'd fallen deeply in love with this amazing man. Phil felt that Justine was special and vowed to stay in touch while he was away.

He returned to Afghanistan for the next six months to complete his duties. Both of them found the long-distance relationship tough, but kept in contact as much as possible.

Justine kept in close touch with Phil's mother and the two of them developed a strong bond and found comfort in each other, as they both missed him so much. Phil's mother felt Justine was perfect for him.

Phil surprised Justine with a phone call one day, asking her to marry him. She couldn't believe it and accepted immediately. She was ecstatic. They agreed to tie the knot when he got back.

Justine

Justine was the youngest of four children. She came from an army background and had spent much of her childhood living in different parts of Europe and the UK because of her father's army job. Her two older brothers had also gone into the military. Justine's parents liked Phil when they met him, but they had doubts at the speed of the engagement. Justine's mother spoke to her about delaying the wedding date, to give her a chance to get to know Phil better. But Justine was determined to go ahead and her parents were willing to support her because they could see how happy she was.

Phil

Phil described his upbringing as a happy one. He was the oldest of three brothers, and became the man of the house when his father died when Phil was 14. He developed a very strong bond with his mother and was very supportive of her. He was often described by teachers as mature beyond his years, and when he joined the army he quickly moved up the ranks, being recognised for his maturity and strong leadership skills. His mother adored Justine and saw her as a perfect match for Phil. She was very happy to hear that he'd proposed to her.

Phil left the army after ten years' service and had only about a week with Justine before their wedding day. They were both excited. Justine described her wedding as the most magical day of her life. She had spent months planning her big day with the help of her parents and Phil's family. Her father walked her down the aisle, she wore her dream dress and everything was perfect.

Crunch Time

After the honeymoon, Justine and Phil moved in temporarily with her parents while they looked for a place together. Phil had some difficulties adjusting to civilian life again, and was also coping with being married. Justine felt happy that she had Phil back permanently in her life, but also felt concerned that he didn't seem that happy.

After a few months, the strain was beginning to show. They had started to bicker about silly little things. Phil had a habit of getting up really early and pacing around downstairs, which woke everyone up. Phil decided to move back in with his mother so that they could have some space from each other. Justine was confused and hurt by this and couldn't reconcile the man she felt she knew with the man who was behaving strangely towards her.

The Way Forward

Justine admitted to her mother that she'd built up a fantasy of what life would be like when she married Phil. She hadn't really thought about what would really happen after the wedding and just hoped things would sort themselves out. Now she felt as though she had to confront the nitty-gritty of everyday life with someone who, at times, felt like a stranger to her.

Phil felt lost after leaving the army. He'd had a clear role, routine and close friends and colleagues who had become like a family unit to him. He felt bereaved without these familiar anchors in his life. Although he had wanted to marry Justine because he loved her deeply, he also wanted to take care of her and provide for her. Living with her parents made him feel useless.

Both of them had built up a fantasy of each other over time. They focused on each other's positive qualities, and filled in the gaps of their long-distance relationship with idealised views of each other. To Phil, Justine represented his future security and permanency once army life was over. To Justine, Phil represented a strong, loving man who made her feel wonderful. The reality of an everyday relationship was proving difficult for both of them.

Although it was clear that Justine and Phil loved each other, they recognised that they needed to get to know each other properly. They made the brave decision to take the pressure off their relationship, and give each other the chance to start to get to know each other fully. They decided to live apart for a few months, and started dating each other.

This really helped them to reconnect with each other, and also gave Phil the space to come to terms with the personal and professional changes in his life.

Having been in the army himself, Justine's father recognised what Phil was going through in adjusting to post-army life, and supported him to get professional help to handle the emotional transitions that he was experiencing.

Over time, with patience, love on both sides and family support, Justine and Phil began to feel positive and stronger in their relationship, and were finally ready to move in together and start their lives as a couple.

———

Meeting someone with whom you have fallen head over heels in love is a wonderfully seductive feeling. Wanting to then marry them as soon as possible can, to some, feel like the next logical step. But it is important to take a step back and examine what is driving your desire to get married so quickly.

EXAMINE YOUR MOTIVES BEFORE YOU JUMP IN
Ask yourself:
- Is getting married my dream coming true?
- Have I had my big day planned out in my head since I was a child?
- Am I focusing on the wedding day itself more than what marriage means to me?
- Does getting married mean that I will feel fulfilled?
- Am I ignoring the advice of family and friends who are warning me to slow down?
- Are family telling me that this is the right person for me?
- Do I feel that this is my last chance to get married?
- Any other additional reasons?

Examine how much you know about your partner. Ask yourself:
- How much do I know about my partner's relationship history?
- How much do I know about my partner's family and friends?
- How much have we discussed our relationship expectations?
- Do I know my partner's views on things that matter to me?
- Do I have a view on what matters most to my partner?

How much do you know about each other as a couple? Ask yourself:

➤ Have we discussed how we would share household chores?
➤ Have we discussed and do we have similar views on starting a family together?
➤ Have we discussed and agreed on who would be the main carer for any children that we may have?
➤ Have we discussed and agreed on money issues?
➤ Have we discussed each other's career ambitions and aspirations?
➤ Have we discussed our religious beliefs?
➤ Have we shared our political views?

Doing this exercise may feel like a very sobering experience, but it is vital that you know exactly what is driving you to tie the knot. By gaining clarity you can then make your decision based on a fuller understanding of your needs, wants and expectations.

DID I MARRY TOO QUICKLY?

You may be in the situation where you have got married very quickly, and now wish you hadn't. This can feel like a deeply lonely and scary place to be.

There is no easy way out of these feelings, but it is important to take stock and first of all be honest with yourself. Rate these key statements on a scale of 1 to 5:
1 = strongly disagree, 5 = strongly agree.

➤ You had lingering doubts before you got married, which you ignored.

➤ You felt trapped shortly after the wedding-day excitement had died down.

➤ You feel as though your partner turned into someone different as soon as you were married.

➤ You feel as though you turned into someone different as soon as you were married.

➤ You avoid spending time with your partner.

➤ You feel unhappy most of the time that you spend with your partner.

➤ The more time you spend with your partner, the more you think that you've made a terrible mistake.

If your answers contain mostly ones and twos, you may be experiencing post-wedding anxiety. This can happen once all the excitement of the wedding day and honeymoon period has passed and the relationship has become more about the nitty-gritty of everyday life. These feelings are entirely normal as you start on the journey of making a life together as a married couple and should fade as you settle into the rhythm of your relationship. It is very possible that all is well and it's more about giving yourself a chance to emotionally readjust to your new status.

What is important at this stage is to check in with yourself and be clear that you married for the right reasons and feel positive about the person you married. This will help you to continue to build a strong relationship foundation.

However, several statements rated three and over may mean that you have been ignoring serious doubts and went ahead with something that you weren't fully sure about.

Self-Help Tips: Addressing Quick-Marriage Problems

1. Take a deep breath and write down the pros and cons of your relationship so far. Notice if the cons list is far longer. Then look at whether the cons are things that are important to you or whether they are nice-to-haves that can be worked on, like wishing your partner would put the toilet seat down.

2. Think through areas where you believe you can work together to make the relationship work better for both of you. That way, you are not approaching your partner with what may appear to be a sudden change of heart, but instead giving them a chance to respond.

3. Have a time frame. Discuss making relationship adjustments that you review one month later to check in and see whether things are improving.

4. Be prepared to give and take. Your partner may also have some things that they feel unsure about. Being open to doing this is the bread and butter of making a relationship work.

5. Sometimes talking to a professional counsellor may help you both gain perspective on your relationship, and you can decide as a couple where you go from here.

6. I know it's not easy, but if after all your efforts you are still struggling, it may signal the end of the road for the relationship. If this is the case, it might be best to agree to end the relationship rather than struggle on in an unhappy situation that is bad for both of you. Swallowing down and denying difficult feelings now will make things harder to challenge and confront the longer you leave it.

WEDDING PLANNING

How you plan, discuss and organise your wedding day can speak volumes about the state of the rest of your relationship. I know I may sound like a spoilsport, but gaining a clear picture of your relationship before you tie the knot will help you to work out where your relationship strengths and challenges lie.

Planning a wedding seems as though it should be a wonderfully positive and unifying experience for you as a couple, but it carries within it many inherent challenges that you may not have anticipated. You could both be blissfully happy about getting married, but when it comes to making wedding decisions together there may be unexpected areas of conflict.

Couples often come a cropper by each party making assumptions about the basic key details: the size of the wedding, the amount of money to spend and who to invite.

Other problems can arise if you assume that you will take on specific roles without discussing them with your partner first. Just imagine if you assume that your partner will sort all transport for the whole family, as well as source the world's best chef to prepare the wedding banquet, and they assume that you will be in charge of the venue and invitations.

Sometimes, one person may feel that they are the only one who is committed to making the wedding day a success, while the other doesn't seem all that interested and only wants to know what time to be at the church!

That's why it is crucial to communicate well to ensure you are both in agreement on what you want from your wedding day.

Sit down with your partner and do this quick quiz. It will help you assess how you plan, manage, discuss and organise this major event in your lives. This way, you will know exactly what the problems are so that you can both take positive steps to improve things.

BEFORE YOU PLAN THE WEDDING

You and your partner should answer these questions separately and then discuss the answers together:

➤ What does the wedding day mean to you?
➤ What do you think it means to your partner?
➤ What does your ideal wedding day look like?
➤ What about your partner?
➤ When discussing the detail of your big day, are you both agreed on:
  • How much to spend.
  • Who to invite.
  • The venue?
➤ Are you both happy to compromise on your ideal wedding if money is tight?
➤ Who is really in control of the wedding day arrangements?
  • Mostly you.
  • Mostly your partner.
  • Mostly your family.
  • Mostly your partner's family.
  • You and your partner share responsibilities?
➤ Does your wedding day feel like it belongs to both of you? If not, why not?

This will really help you to work out how you communicate, negotiate and compromise on key issues. If you discover that you need to communicate more openly and honestly with each other, then now's the time to do it. (Doing the communication exercise on page 103 will help you achieve this.)

WEDDINGS AND YOUR FAMILIES

Parents often want to get involved with wedding day preparations, and some want to be included every step of the way. In fact, conflict with family over wedding plans is incredibly common. Even the most calm and peaceful of families can suddenly come up with demands.

There is no doubt that your wedding will expose a mixture of feelings, reactions and behaviours in your parents and parents-in-law.

There will be some parents who are collaborative, others who are distant and some who are boiling over with such enthusiasm that they want to take over completely. Planning a wedding is stressful enough without the additional pressure of feeling as though you have to please everybody. If roles are clearly identified and agreed upon, the wedding planning is much more likely to go smoothly. However, problems occur when communication about who is responsible for what is unclear or vague and boundaries aren't set. This leaves room for potential power struggles to ensue between you, your partner and your respective families.

There may be conflicts about how much to spend, what type of venue to have, whom to invite and the style of wedding. The list of potential problems is endless! For some, it is traditional for the bride's family to pay for the wedding and, even today, when the couple themselves might be paying, the bride's family might still want more control, and the groom's family may then feel left out. Other emotional issues can come when either family feel that they are losing their child to the spouse and there can be competition between the mother-in-law and the bride. Jealousies can even emerge between parents and in-laws about who is more involved and therefore more important, and competition to outdo each other is not uncommon … You may be left wondering, whose wedding is it anyway?!

And, sometimes, no matter how clearly things are laid out, there may still be a family member who continuously tries to take control. All these aspects can add extra stress, on you individually and on your relationship, and can make what should be a happy event feel emotionally fraught.

———

Case Study: Don't Interfere

Nathan (32) and Maeve (28) had been living together for two and a half years when he proposed to her while they were on holiday. She happily accepted. They decided on a date, which gave them six months to organise their special day. They were agreed on where to get married, who to invite and how much to spend.

Both their families were delighted and offered to help. It was agreed that both families would contribute equal amounts of money for their wedding day, and that they would be available to step in whenever they were needed.

Maeve

Maeve grew up in a large family – she was the middle child of six. She had sustained a serious injury from a car accident when she was five and had to have her leg amputated from the knee down. She'd endured many hospital visits and operations throughout her childhood, and was given a prosthetic leg. Her parents were determined that she would grow up to feel secure and loved and to be independent-minded. Maeve was treated no differently to her siblings because of her disability and she developed a resilient attitude and never thought of herself as needing special treatment by others.

When she met Nathan, she was open and honest with him about her leg right from the start and showed him what her body looked like without her prosthetic leg. Nathan was incredibly loving and supportive and told her that he loved her even more.

Nathan

Nathan was the youngest of three brothers. He came from a close loving family and described his childhood as very happy and comfortable. His two older brothers were much older than him and Nathan felt as though he was on only child because by the time he was eight both his brothers had left home to go to college. Both his brothers were now married with families of their own and both had moved some distance away from where they were brought up. Nathan still lived fairly close to his parents' home.

He maintained a close relationship with both his parents, although sometimes felt that his mother still treated him like the baby of the family who needed her support.

Crunch Time

Once they'd shared their good news with family, problems began to emerge between Nathan's mother, Suzanne, and Maeve. Maeve and Suzanne had so far had a reasonably good relationship, they spoke on the phone and saw each other fairly regularly. However, since the proposal, Maeve felt that Suzanne had changed almost overnight, becoming pushy and rude.

Suzanne had started turning up at their home with what she described as appropriate wedding dress choices for Maeve that would cover up her legs. She also offered more money for a bigger and better venue. She constantly mentioned how embarrassed she felt by the small venue that they'd chosen for their reception.

Maeve started to feel undermined and stressed out and spoke to Nathan about it. He felt strongly that his mother was just trying to help out. However, Maeve felt that Suzanne was infantilising her and she felt patronised.

The atmosphere between the two women became so bad that Nathan knew he couldn't ignore it any more. Although he felt uncomfortable, Nathan finally spoke to his mother about her behaviour. Suzanne broke down and complained that Maeve was pushing her out of the biggest event in her son's life and couldn't understand Maeve's sudden hostility towards her.

The breakdown in communication between Maeve and Suzanne was causing so much negativity and affecting the whole family. Maeve felt that any pleasure she'd had in planning the wedding with Nathan was being drained away by Suzanne's attitude. She felt so awful that she even considered cancelling the wedding altogether. Nathan felt caught between his mother and his fiancée and didn't want to upset either of them. However, he knew that things couldn't carry on as they were, and he finally admitted to Maeve that his mother's domineering behaviour sometimes left him feeling helpless as to how to handle her. But, he didn't want his mother to spoil things for him and Maeve and he finally stepped in to support her.

The Way Forward

Maeve suggested that this was something that she and Suzanne needed to resolve themselves and proposed that the two of them went out for lunch and talk through how to sort things out.

Suzanne was very honest and shared that she felt as though she was losing her little boy and that she had been feeling overemotional about it. All she was trying to do was to help make it the best day of their lives, but felt pushed out.

Maeve told Suzanne that she felt that for the first time in their relationship she was so angry with her because Suzanne seemed to be treating her not as an equal but as someone with a disability who couldn't cope, was useless and needed help.

This conversation helped both of them to understand how hurt the other person was feeling and what was causing the rift between them.

Nathan and Maeve wanted Suzanne to feel included and they agreed that she would be in charge of organising the catering and the flowers. However, they were both agreed that they would stand firm that they didn't need Suzanne to give them more money and that she would leave Maeve to choose her own wedding gown without interference. This clarity helped Suzanne to feel included and to know where the boundaries were, and ensured that their wedding day was as they wanted it.

———

Handling family members can be a very tricky affair, but it can be done with minimum emotional drama if you and your partner are agreed on what you both want and are prepared to be very clear with family about how you visualise your special day. I remember sitting down with my mother and enthusiastically describing to her my plans for a small, intimate wedding celebration – something that my partner and I had discussed and really wanted. I watched her face go from fit to burst with excitement to absolute horror. She then offered to ship in 300 of her closest friends to make up the numbers! I remember thinking that if I gave in to her now, then she'll forever be inviting 300 of her closest friends to everything I did.

Self-Help Tips: Managing Family Members

1. Reduce the stress by being clear with each other about what kind of wedding you both want.
2. Agree and stick to a budget. This will help you to prioritise, stay focused and maintain control.
3. Make a list of guests whom you both want to invite and agree numbers.
4. Be sensitive to parental and in-law needs, so that they feel included, and play to their strengths. If, for example, your mum has great organisational skills, then give her the role of organising the seating plan.
5. If you want to have your wedding day in your own unique way, then be honest with family and say so – don't be tempted to be a crowd pleaser.
6. Being firm but fair with family now will set the tone for your future relationship with them. If you give in to the needs of others at this point, you'll find that you will be giving in to demands for the rest of your relationship.
7. Make sure you and your partner operate as a team and always have each other's backs so that you protect your relationship from the demands of others.

The wedding day is a signal that you and your partner want to celebrate your relationship commitment to each other, surrounded by those you love. But there are challenges that come with the joy and these can vary from feeling as though your special day has been hijacked by family expectations to worrying that your partner is not all that interested in helping you organise the big day. Deciding as a couple what matters most to both of you is the best place to start. This will help reduce tensions and conflicts with the wider family and help you get perspective on what really matters. The wedding day is just that – one moment in time to symbolise your love for each other. It is important not to freeze-frame the wedding day as the template on which to build a life together. Marriage is the on-going commitment journey that needs both of you to be fully invested in order to make it work.

Making a commitment to the person you love and with whom you want to spend the rest of your life is a wonderful feeling and a big deal. However, it is so important that you and your partner are agreed on your reasons for making this powerful commitment. Addressing any doubts and concerns sooner rather than later will ensure that you are not storing up heartbreak for yourselves further down the line. Being open and honest with one another will ensure that you both know where you stand and you are getting married with the best intentions on both sides. This means that you will set the right tone for the rest of your relationship when it comes to handling both the good and the challenging times.

Chapter 6
Starting a Family

The decision to start a family can be exciting, daunting and very possibly bring up a wealth of other conflicting feelings. We may long to recreate the wonderful childhood that we had or may want to ensure that we are the best and most loving parents so that we become nothing like our own neglectful folks. We may worry about not being perfect parents or may simply hope for the best.

From wondering whether you're ready to have kids, if you can get pregnant in the first place or how many kids to have, or whether you don't want any at all or want to adopt – all these thoughts and feelings need proper expression and discussion within your relationship with your partner.

Having a child, or even deciding that children aren't for you, is the start of a journey that is going to bring into sharp focus your core beliefs, your life script, your childhood, your relationship with your own parents (whether they're living or not), your hopes and dreams, and your anxieties. All these feelings jostling for your attention are completely normal and it is vital to acknowledge them, because they'll all help to inform you of your next step.

In this chapter I am going to help you to take a step-by-step approach to working through this life-changing decision and to help you work out what is best for you and your partner; whether it is embarking on the journey of having your first child or choosing not to have any children at all.

I will focus on both the positive and the challenging changes in identity, intimacy, your partnership dynamic and your parenting style, which you will become more aware of once you start a family. I will also look at what may happen in your relationship when a baby does come along and offer tips on how to positively handle the emotional changes that this will inevitably bring about.

Let's say that, so far, your relationship is going wonderfully well and you both look at each other one day and decide to go for it and start a family.

What you both bring to the table are a number of hopes, expectations and dreams of how your family will be. These will be shaped by your own experiences growing up, your values and beliefs about parenthood that may have been influenced by your primary care givers or other significant parental figures in your life.

You may also have made a number of assumptions about how the relationship with your partner will look and feel once a baby comes along, based on how the relationship with your partner has been so far. This may be a good indicator, but having a child changes everything and brings about increased stress, unpredictability and big emotional challenges. Stress like this can have us reverting back to our default setting during times of difficulty, which can add extra tension and pressure to our relationships.

My partner and I had a happy and secure relationship when we decided to have a family. My pregnancy progressed well with no real problems and even the birth was fairly uncomplicated. However, our daughter became sick and had to go into hospital when she was just a few weeks old. To say we as new parents were terrified would be an understatement.

Every ounce of our relationship was tested. We both went back to our default settings: I got angry with him because he was so calm and measured. I couldn't understand how he could be like this, especially when neither of us knew what was happening to our baby. He got frustrated with me because, in my heightened anxious state, I ambushed every doctor I laid eyes on and demanded a second, third and fourth opinion.

We both had to draw on our inner strength and work together as a team to handle the crisis, which fortunately had a positive outcome and our daughter was absolutely fine. This became our first real lesson in relationship resilience.

So, whether you are thinking of adopting, using a surrogate or having the baby yourself, I think it is so important to do your own pre-baby evaluation to ensure that you are both emotionally on the same page, can assess the strength and resilience that you have in your relationship so far and also so that you both have the opportunity to voice any concerns or doubts that may be lurking under the surface.

This quick exercise will help you both to explore feelings, thoughts, core beliefs, and attitudes about what becoming a parent really means to you as an individual and as a couple. It can also really help you assess if you or your partner don't want to have children at all.

PRE-BABY EVALUATION

1. About how you feel right now:
➤ When you begin thinking about having a baby, how do you imagine life will change for you?
➤ How positive on a scale of 1–10 do you feel about becoming a parent? (1 = not positive at all; 10 = very positive.) *Anything 5 and under needs to be explored. You may be feeling unsure and these feelings need to be voiced.*

➤ How do you feel on a scale of 1–10 about becoming a parent, where 1 is very negative and 10 is very positive? *Anything 5 and under needs to be explored.*

➤ Give three positive words that come to mind when you think about parenthood.

➤ Give three negative words that come to mind when you think about parenthood.

➤ What do you hope to gain by having a baby?

➤ What do you fear losing by having a baby?

➤ How do you think you will change as a person by having a baby?

➤ How do you think your partner will change?

➤ If you found out you were pregnant today, how do you think you'd react and how do you think your partner would react?

➤ How many children do you imagine you will have five years/ten years from now?

➤ How many children do you want?

➤ How many children does your partner want?

2. About your past:

➤ How would you describe your parents' relationship?

➤ How would you describe the atmosphere you grew up in?
  • Warm.
  • Secure.
  • Distant.
  • Strict.
  • Lots of hugs.
  • Few boundaries.
  • Lots of rules.
  • Cold.

➤ How do you think this atmosphere may have influenced you?

➤ What did you learn from your parents about parenting?

➤ What three things did they teach you about parenthood that you would like to emulate?

➤ What three things did you experience from them about parenting that you never want to repeat as a parent yourself?

3. About you and your partner:

➤ Looking at your relationship right now, how happy do you feel with your partner?

➤ If there are any challenges that you have faced in the past six months/one year, have you resolved them positively and constructively?

➤ Are there any doubts you have about your partner's ability to become a parent that concern you? Have you voiced these concerns?

➤ Do you have any concerns about your own ability to become a parent? Have you shared these concerns with your partner?

➤ When you reflect on the time that you and your partner have had together, would you say that you have made the best of your relationship so far before starting the journey of having a baby?

4. Parenting messages from the past that may influence parenting style:

➤ When you imagine your partner as a parent, what positive qualities do you think they have that will make them a good parent?

➤ When you imagine yourself as a parent, what positive qualities do you think you have that will make you a good parent?

➤ Are there any concerns your partner has about their own upbringing that may get in the way of them being able to parent well?

➤ Are there any concerns you have about your upbringing that may get in the way of you being able to parent well?

➤ What significant parenting messages from your past do you think will influence your parenting style?

➤ What significant parenting messages from your partner's past do you think will influence your partner's parenting style?

5. Reality check:

These are tough questions to ask yourself but are absolutely worth doing as they'll help you identify your motivations for parenthood. Ask yourself:

➤ Am I starting a family in order to feel secure?

➤ Would having a child provide me with someone to love?

➤ Am I following my friends' decision to have a family now?

➤ Am I bowing to the pressure of family expectations to start a family when I'm really not sure?

➤ Do I have serious doubts about starting a family?

➤ Is starting a family a priority for both of us?

➤ Does my partner want a family more than I do?

➤ Do I want a family more than my partner does?

➤ Are we both willing to give up our freedom/lifestyle or are we not prepared to?

➤ Am I prepared for my/my partner's body to change? Is my partner prepared for my/their body to change?

And if you are to be the one who stays at home:

➤ How will I feel if I have to give up work?

➤ Am I prepared to lose my status at work?

➤ Will I feel helpless, alone and vulnerable at home with a baby?

➤ Have I got other support, like friends or family, in addition to my partner?

6. How involved do you want to be?

➤ We will both be hands-on parents.

➤ I will be the main carer.

➤ My partner will be the main carer.

➤ We'll need a full-time nanny.

➤ The baby will go to a baby-sitter/nursery because I'll have to work.

➤ I don't expect my partner to be that involved.

➤ We will both bathe, cuddle, feed and change the baby.

These questions help you assess where you're both at from an emotional and practical perspective. Having a baby is a huge emotional, psychological and practical shift, and it is never too soon to start exploring how life will change and whether you are mentally, physically and financially prepared for that change. Of course you can't prepare for every eventuality, because life is too unpredictable and tends to throw us a curve ball when we least expect it. However, the better prepared you are, the more resilient you will be to handle the challenges that will come up.

Working through these questions will also help you and your partner to open up about any fears and concerns that you may have about becoming parents. It is very natural to feel apprehensive and a little bit scared – so it's vital that you both feel safe to express true feelings early on.

If you've worked through this exercise and feel that you are both on the same page and can't wait to get started, then that's great news. However, if you are not on the same page, there could be other feelings and emotional roadblocks that may pose even greater challenges.

EMOTIONAL AND PRACTICAL CHALLENGES

All kinds of factors can shape our decision to start a family. There could be practical considerations that make you uncertain of how exactly to move forward such as: money worries, illness or lack of space. And emotional considerations like: not being in synchrony with our partner, family pressures, fear of loss of status, worrying about physical changes, emotional upheaval, coping with miscarriage, dealing with lesbian/gay/bisexual/ transgender issues, role conflict, different attachment styles and different expectations. There are many issues that can have a knock-on effect on how you may approach parenthood.

FAMILY CONFLICT

Having a baby throws up new emotional and practical challenges when it comes to your respective families that perhaps you may not have thought about much beforehand. For instance, how much involvement from parents and in-laws would be okay for both of you? You may not want any input from family members, while your partner may want to include their family in everything. Or your parents may see fit to drop in whenever they want in order to help out with the baby and your partner may find this infuriating.

There is absolutely no doubt that support with a new baby is vital. Being clear about what help you would like, when you'd like that support and who from is the key to gaining the best help for your new family unit.

That's why it is so important to discuss with your partner who you want in your support network and how you want it to work for both of you. It is useful to do this before having your child, as well as afterwards. Being flexible and reassessing your support network is important once your child is born, as some family members (and friends) may not be as keen as you'd anticipated, and others more so. Doing this will go a long way to ensuring that you don't feel intruded upon, stifled or even neglected.

———

Case Study: Now or Never

Martin (40) a financial advisor and Julia (39) a freelance photographer, met and fell in love very quickly. Both described themselves as not being on the lookout for a relationship, when they bumped into each other at a party. Julia had just come out of a long-term relationship, which ended when her ex had told her that he didn't want to have a family with her. She was totally devastated by this, because for the past year they'd been making plans to move in together and take the relationship to the next level. Julia had been off men since her ex and had resigned herself to never having children because she felt she was getting too old for motherhood.

Martin had been single for the last six months and had been enjoying himself on the dating scene. He wasn't looking for anything long term and was happy to play the field for a while. He had previously been married for a couple of years in his late twenties, but the marriage had ended because both of them admitted that they'd got married too quickly and neither of them was ready to start a family. They separated amicably and had since stayed friends.

Julia and Martin enjoyed a whirlwind romance. They described having so much in common. She felt comfortable allowing him into her life and he, for the first time in a long time, felt as though this could be the woman he would spend the rest of his life with. Although they'd talked about having children, neither of them had really focused on this as a real possibility. Julia often joked that she was too old for motherhood now. So it came as a complete shock when she discovered she was pregnant. Julia described feeling both elated and terrified as she'd given up hope of becoming a mother. Martin was over the moon and immediately informed his parents that they were going to be grandparents.

The first real source of tension came when they were deciding where to live before the baby arrived. Martin wanted Julia to move in with him; she felt that his place was too small. In the end, Martin moved into Julia's house. At seven months pregnant, Julia took control of the wedding arrangements and told Martin that he didn't have to do much, but simply show up on the day. Within a year of meeting they were married and had had their first child.

Although Julia and Martin were incredibly happy to welcome their son into their lives, their relationship had gone through a huge metamorphosis. At the point at which they were finding out how to live with each other, Julia was going through pregnancy and dealing with her changing body and changing moods. Their sex life changed and Martin often worried that during sex he may be harming the baby in some way. Martin had also been used to his own space, and coming home whenever he liked. Suddenly finding himself a dad-to-be, and living in Julia's home, he discovered the rules had changed. Julia expected him to be home at a certain time or at least tell her when he was coming home. Martin found her need to know his movements and whereabouts frustrating. He worried that she didn't trust him. These issues were temporarily put to one side once their son was born.

Crunch Time

Problems started to flare up again when Martin invited his parents to stay with them for a couple of weeks to help Julia out with the baby. He hadn't checked this with her, but had felt that once he returned to work she could do with extra help. His parents, who were both retired, had offered to come and stay. This had caused Julia to lose her temper. She'd planned to employ a part-time nanny right from the start so that she could carry on working from home. Martin saw this as a waste of money, particularly as his parents could step in whenever they needed. The two of them started to argue constantly.

Julia

Julia was the youngest of four children and had experienced a very turbulent childhood. Her parents had divorced when she was just eight years old. They had joint custody of the children and she found herself constantly moving between their two homes. She often felt as though she, as the youngest, was a weapon in a very fraught power struggle between the two of them. She asked to live with her dad permanently when she was ten. Her two older brothers already lived with him, as Julia's mother had found them too difficult to manage. However, since he had remarried, his new wife didn't want another child in the family. As a result, Julia saw less and less of her dad over time and she ended up living with her mother and older sister – an arrangement she described as awful. Her mother and older sister argued constantly, often pulling Julia into the rows, and she felt caught in the middle. Julia didn't have much to do with her family any more and described having strong friendships – these were people she felt she could really trust and rely on, unlike her family whom she didn't trust at all.

She hadn't invited her parents or her siblings to her wedding, nor did she want them involved in her son's life.

Martin

Martin came from a very close-knit family. He was the oldest of four, having two sisters and a brother. He described his childhood as happy, secure and comfortable. He experienced his parents as supportive and loving and always ready to help any of their children out if they needed them. Martin grew up thinking everyone's family was like his own, although he described himself as a bit sheltered. He had pretty loose boundaries with his family and they would often just drop by for a visit unannounced. This was normal and acceptable in their family dynamic and he longed to create a similar environment within his new family. He wanted his parents to be involved in every step of his son's life and wanted Julia to integrate into his family and have the loving support that he felt she truly deserved.

The Way Forward

Julia and Martin knew that they needed support to handle the emotional challenges that they now faced. They felt, however, that they were at odds with each other and neither felt able to compromise. Julia knew that becoming a parent triggered a lot of emotions from her past about feeling caught in the middle of a battle and often unwanted by her parents. She wanted her son to feel the opposite of what she'd felt – she wanted him to feel loved by her every second of every day. This made her appear controlling and uncompromising. Martin was overwhelmed by the feelings of love he felt for his son and just wanted to include his family in that loving glow. He felt that he'd benefited so much from having a positive family, and wanted his son to have the same experience. This made him dig his heels in with Julia – and he stuck to his position about his parents coming to stay.

Both had their own emotional agendas, but neither had felt ready to express them.

Martin's parents arrived to stay for a fortnight and the tensions increased. It was Martin's mother who helped broker an honest conversation between the two of them. She realised that Martin had invited them to stay without Julia's consent and could see clearly what was happening.

Martin's parents were able to offer emotional and practical support that gave Julia and Martin the time and space to take a step back and look at what was happening. They agreed to have extra support, with a part-time childminder so that Julia could work. They admitted that they were both overwhelmed with life-changing events, were still getting to know each other and needed help to work through this.

They agreed to have a few sessions of brief, focused counselling to help them work through immediate challenges in a constructive way. And Julia decided to have individual counselling to handle issues from her own past that had arisen since becoming a parent.

————

Self-Help Tips: To Ensure You Have Enough Support

Having a baby is a massive emotional transition and the more support you have, the better. It is so true that it really does take a village to raise a child.

1. Make sure that you do have support for yourself, especially in the first few weeks. Your health visitor and GP can be an invaluable resource for this. A baby is a round-the-clock emotional and physical challenge. If there are family members or close friends who can step in and help, then welcome them in. This gives you the opportunity to get much-needed rest.

2. Ensure that you get out of the house and get fresh air. This can get rid of that cabin-fever overwhelmed feeling and help get you into a more positive frame of mind.

3. Don't isolate yourself. Join groups where you can mix with other new parents. This can be a big support and mutual help.

4. Build in adult time for you and your partner. This may seem like a chore, but it is so important. Even an hour a week where you just sit down with each other and share how you're doing will help keep you emotionally connected to each other.

5. If you find that there are other deeper issues getting in your way, then talking to a counsellor can be a big help.

PERFECT PARENTING

It is natural to want to do everything right, be the best you can for your baby and to have everything all sorted out. But sometimes this type of perfectionist thinking can be an emotional trap where you may be unwittingly putting too much pressure on yourself to be the perfect parent, perfect partner and perfect homemaker all at once. If you're trying to be perfect at all times then you will inevitably wear yourself out and add unnecessary stress to an already exhausting situation. The truth is, it doesn't matter if the house is not pristine or that there are dishes on the worktop, or if when people come round you're just wearing an old tracksuit! This is totally normal when your priorities have changed and you are focusing on your baby's needs.

Case Study: The Scheduled Couple

Jeff (38) and Lisa (36) both worked as accountants and had been married for five years when they decided to start a family. They felt that their relationship was strong enough at this point to embrace a new member of the family. They decided that Lisa would start working part-time once she fell pregnant and would take a year off to be a full-time mum when the baby came along. They agreed that after this time she'd put the baby into childcare so that she could return to her job full-time.

They were both very happy with this plan of action and Lisa got pregnant very quickly. But she had terrible morning sickness for the first four months and found it very difficult to work at all. At six months Lisa was told that she had pre-eclampsia and had to have bed rest and medical monitoring. Although Jeff was very supportive, he felt increasing concern that Lisa's health was suffering.

Crunch Time
When their daughter finally arrived, Jeff and Lisa were feeling completely stressed out. Fears about Lisa's health had left Jeff feeling helpless, anxious and panicky. Although both their families lived some distance away, Lisa's mother offered to move in for a couple of weeks to help them out. Lisa declined the offer saying that they had everything under control and Jeff went back to work two weeks after Rachel was born. Lisa found this incredibly difficult and felt lonely at times. She hardly went out and she discouraged friends from visiting her because she didn't feel organised enough.

For the first three months after the birth of her daughter, Lisa felt depressed and vulnerable. She found it hard to admit that she wasn't coping all that well and didn't feel able to ask for help. She had a long-held belief about motherhood and felt that she should know what she was doing. That she simply had to get on with it.

The Way Forward

On a visit to the family, the health visitor sat down with Lisa and Jeff and asked them how they were. Both exhausted and feeling stressed out, they opened up to her. They admitted struggling to cope, and that with life no longer having any kind of regular pattern it seemed to be spiralling out of their control.

They agreed that they both needed help to sort out how to cope with the changes.

Lisa

Lisa recognised that she hated asking for help and had almost always been the person people turned to for advice and support. She saw herself as someone who was one of life's copers and had a can-do approach to problems.

Lisa was an only child who described her childhood as a happy one. Her parents doted on her and were positive and encouraging. When Lisa was about ten, her parents noticed that she had a very pedantic streak. She always wanted to do things properly and often felt uncomfortable if rules weren't being followed to the letter.

When she started her first job, this behaviour manifested itself more acutely. She was very thorough and careful in her work, which meant that she sometimes took longer than she needed to finish off tasks. This aspect of her hadn't really intruded negatively on her life until she got pregnant.

Although she had lots of friends and a supportive family, she had been unwilling to reveal to anyone that she was having difficulty handling the practical and emotional upheavals. Lack of sleep and a difficult pregnancy coupled with an unwillingness to ask for help had all been factors that had contributed to her depression.

Just by talking her feelings through with the health visitor, Lisa began to see that trying to deny her emotions had led to her feeling much worse. Lisa recognised that asking for help was critical to her well-being and would also give her the opportunity to bond with her baby in the way that she wanted to. Lisa finally invited her mum to stay over for a couple of weeks to help them out. She built in time to get out and see friends and share how she was feeling. Having extra support meant that she didn't feel isolated and she realised that other new mothers felt similar to her at times. Sharing these feelings really helped her to move forward.

Jeff

Jeff was the oldest of two children – he had a younger sister. He described his upbringing as ordered and predictable. His father was a nurse in a hospital who mainly worked on the night shift. Jeff's mother had chosen to give up her job as a research scientist to concentrate on raising her children.

Jeff described how his mother always had everything organised at home and that she worked hard to maintain a calm atmosphere so that the children weren't noisy and boisterous while their father slept during the afternoon. However, sometimes when simple things did go wrong, whether it was the milk not being delivered on time or the electricity going out, Jeff remembers witnessing his mother getting very panicky and anxious. If he or his sister sometimes got too loud and out of control while playing, Jeff's mother would almost be in tears as she tried to calm them down. He described hating seeing his mother like this, because she was usually so together. As he grew up, he found that whenever people were emotional around him, or expressed difficult feelings, he just wanted to run away and hide.

Jeff recognised that he often felt uncomfortable when things didn't go to plan, so when Lisa had suffered during the pregnancy he found it hard to deal with. By burying himself in work, he'd hoped that life would just go back to normal after a while. When this didn't happen and Lisa became depressed, Jeff felt frustrated and helpless.

Jeff and Lisa had struggled to let go of their scheduled approach and the arrival of their daughter had tested this to the limit. Jeff realised that the more he tried to go back to the way things were, the more challenging life became, and he slowly learnt to compromise and build in flexibility. He recognised also that sharing how he felt mattered too, and this enabled them to work as a team to handle the challenges together.

Self-Help Tips: Ditching Perfectionism and Being a Good-Enough Parent

1. A difficult pregnancy is challenging and it is so important to get the right support to manage it. Whether it is talking to your partner, midwife, parents, friends or a counsellor, the more support you have the better you will feel.

2. For such a small bundle of joy, your baby wields an enormous amount of power and is going to challenge all aspects of your life. Holding on to the way things were and hoping your baby will just slot in is a fantasy. Let go of that belief right now.

3. As a family, build in a routine wherever you can – feeding time, bath time, going for a regular walk. This will create some sense of order, but be prepared to be flexible. This will ease the tension.

4. Prioritise bonding with your baby over a messy kitchen. This time with your baby is precious, and you won't have this special time again with them. This is your time to create a positive and enduring attachment with your baby.

POST-NATAL DEPRESSION

Studies suggest that 50 per cent of women in the Western world experience baby blues – feeling low and out of sorts – and that these feelings tend to disappear on their own.

However, for some women this can turn into post-natal depression, and according to NHS statistics this affects about one in seven mothers in the UK.[6] If this is you, then here is what you must do. You must not suffer in silence, nor must you feel like you've failed in some way. You should not feel guilty about not being the world's best mum because other mothers are telling you how wonderfully easy motherhood is. Don't believe a word of it – motherhood is a challenge whoever you are! Pregnancy and having a baby is up there on the high-stress-factors list along with divorce, bereavement and moving house![7]

If you are concerned that you might be suffering from depression talk to your partner, health visitor and/or close friends about how you feel.

Keeping a diary of how you feel can be a challenge when you have a baby to handle and might be feeling sleep deprived, so use the 'Post-it method'. Just put down how you're feeling (no more than three or four key words that nail it for you) on a Post-it each day for two weeks. Something like 'tired, sad, lonely' or 'upbeat, optimistic, exhausted'. This will help you notice a pattern of how you are feeling. This will also act as a reminder to share these feelings with your support network – partner, family, friends, health visitor or GP. It is a quick and easy way to flag up how you are doing so that you can get the support you need.

The sooner you can get the right support and help, the better for you and for your family.

PARENTING STYLES

It might seem too soon to start thinking about what your parenting style may be before your baby is even born, but it isn't! You may not realise it, but you already have a model of parenting. You have already learnt from and are influenced by your own parents or parental figures whether you are consciously aware of it or not. These internalised messages influence how you may bring up your own children in many different ways, including your beliefs about right and wrong; how to discipline; loose, firm or no boundaries; and whether you hug your children or not. Some people may be very conscious of not wanting to be anything like their own parents when it comes to raising children, and work hard to do the opposite of their parents; while others may believe that the way they were brought up was absolutely the best way, and therefore wish to bring up their own children in a very similar way themselves. You and your partner may have similar or very different views and values about how to raise a family.

The key is to become aware of your parenting style in order to compromise so that you can create a consistent message for your child. Conflicting approaches can cause tension between parents and is a common source of dispute.

Studies describe three broad categories of parenting style:

➤ **The authoritarian.** Key message: the disciplinarian, I am right. My way or no way.
➤ **The laissez-faire.** Key message: more lenient, laid-back, doesn't tend to tell children off for doing wrong, more permissive and often few or no boundaries.
➤ **The authoritative.** Key message: firm but fair, encouraging but within set limits. Structured and loving.

The authoritative approach is considered to be the best approach. Imagine that you are the parent who is more laid-back and happy not to enforce rules, is happy to discuss and negotiate most things with your children from bedtime to what to have for dinner. But your partner believes that children should be seen and not heard, that they should always do as they're told and that their word as parent is final. This would cause major problems as you and your partner pull in different directions. This would also be terribly confusing to your children, as they'd struggle to work out which parental messages to follow.

Confusion like this can leave room for children to become manipulative – playing one parent against another, or taking sides with one parent and innocently becoming the confidante – or feeling stuck in a tug-of-love.

YOUR PARENTING STYLE AS A COUPLE
It is important to understand and review your style and that of your partner's.

Draw up a list of what qualities you both want to instil in your child.

For example, we want our child to be:

➤ Friendly.
➤ Outgoing.
➤ Kind.
➤ Confident.
➤ Sociable, and so on.

Then discuss with your partner what both of you would do to help your child achieve these qualities. E.g.:

➤ Showing love.
➤ Modelling kindness.
➤ Lots of hugs.
➤ Give them firm boundaries, and so on.

By being child focused in this way, you and your partner can start to look at how you can work together to provide the environment that will give your child love and consistency. If your styles are different, this also gives you and your partner an excellent opportunity to discuss where you can meet in the middle.

If there are distinct areas of difference, and your approaches too conflicting, then there's absolutely nothing wrong with talking to a professional about how the two of you can work together in order to provide a consistent parenting style.

LESBIAN, GAY, BISEXUAL AND TRANSGENDER (LGBT) RELATIONSHIPS AND PARENTING

In a heterosexually skewed world, where it is wrongly assumed that parental figures are about having a mum and a dad, people in the LGBT community need positive and supportive advice. The amount of issues to think about can seem very daunting, whether it is discussing how to have the baby or who will carry the baby, to thinking about how to handle prejudices from the outside world. Thankfully there is a growing amount of excellent advice to help you and your partner handle the complexities. My focus here is on the psychological, emotional and practical aspects of starting a family. However, it is crucial to also take advice on medical and legal issues as well.

―――――

Case Study: The Time is Now

Anna (31) and Stella (40) had been together for five years. Anna worked as an actress and Stella ran her own cafe. They described their relationship as very happy. They'd travelled the world, enjoyed a comfortable lifestyle and had lots of friends. Recently, Anna had started to think about motherhood and felt that having a family would make their relationship complete. While talking things through one evening, Anna shared these feelings with Stella. Stella had always been open to the idea of having children at some point in the future, but Anna now felt a sense of urgency about starting a family.

Ian, a close male friend of theirs had often said that he'd happily be their sperm donor, but the conversation had never gone further than that. Anna decided to invite him over for dinner to discuss it more seriously. Although Stella adored Ian, she wasn't entirely sure that they should talk to him until they had given themselves a chance to fully think things through. Stella worried about the fact that they hadn't even discussed the fundamentals: who would get pregnant? Was this going to be artificial insemination? Was Ian going to co-parent with them or not? What were his expectations?

Stella kept her feelings to herself for fear that she'd upset Anna. Although the two of them loved each other very much, Stella was used to putting Anna's needs before her own and often compared living with Anna to living with an over-affectionate child with boundless energy whose charm was irresistible.

Crunch Time

At the dinner, Ian was very supportive and felt very honoured to be asked. He had questions of his own and stated that although he was very happy to help them out, he felt that the three of them really needed to spend some more time thinking it through.

A couple of days later, Stella broached the subject with Anna. She suggested that the way things were work-wise, it would fall to Anna to have the baby and stop working, while Stella would be the main earner. Anna felt resentful that Stella automatically assumed that Anna would carry the baby.

This caused tension between them and brought into sharp focus their differing approaches to handling problems. Stella felt strongly that whenever she didn't automatically go along with what Anna wanted, Anna would become defensive and angry. Anna felt that Stella often assumed that she was incapable of grown-up decisions and sometimes as a result became hyper-controlling.

Stella spoke to a close friend of hers about the problems she and Anna were having. Her friend recommended a therapist whom she knew had an excellent understanding of LGBT issues and what they were currently grappling with. At their early sessions, the counsellor helped them see that they both wanted to be parents, but there were currently some emotional barriers getting in their way.

Anna

Anna grew up as an only child brought up by her single mother. Anna's mother had a brief fling with someone when she was 19, and when she found out that she was pregnant, she decided to keep the baby and bring it up herself. Growing up, Anna and her mother had a very close bond. When Anna was in her late teens, people often thought that she and her mother were sisters. They had a very strong connection and Anna admired her mother's strength to bring her into the world and nurture her single-handedly.

When Anna came out to her mother she was very supportive and encouraging and went all out to educate herself and be there for her daughter. She wanted to be part of her lifestyle and sometimes hung out with Anna's friends. This meant that, at times, the boundaries with mother and daughter were blurred, and Anna felt her mother was over-intrusive at times. However, she also saw her as her role model who had helped her develop confidence and a strong sense of self: if Anna wanted something, she had no problem with going all out to get it. This positive quality, however, meant that sometimes Anna would become pushy and refuse to hear another point of view if she didn't like what she was being told. This aspect of her behaviour sometimes manifested itself in her relationship with Stella.

Stella

Stella described her childhood as difficult. Her parents weren't particularly close and the intimacy had gone out of their relationship a long time previously. She clearly remembers that her parents never hugged or kissed each other, and they barely spoke. She had one older brother who had left home when Stella was ten. She described the atmosphere in her house as stifling, and she longed to escape like her brother had done. Her father would sometimes confide in her and tell her what a miserable marriage he was in and warned her to never get married. When Stella was in her teens, she described how her mother completely emotionally disappeared and she took on the role of being her father's emotional crutch. Stella remembered telling him that she was a lesbian when she was 18 and just about to leave home and go to college. This was met with hardly a flicker from her father, who only seemed to want to focus on rebuilding his own life and moving on from his lifeless marriage. He saw Stella leaving home as the completion of his job as a parent and the beginning of his own adventure. This lack of support left Stella feeling angry and from then on she had very little to do with her parents.

Through subsequent sessions, Anna and Stella explored what roles they undertook in their relationship. Stella admitted that she sometimes experienced Anna as a child and was fearful that a baby would mean she would become the parent of two. She also feared that she had the potential to emotionally check-out and abandon her family in the way that her mother had done. She recognised that she'd also refused to assert herself in the relationship and tended to give in to Anna, for fear that Anna might leave her.

Anna felt stifled at times with Stella, believing that Stella often wanted to prevent her from being spontaneous. Although she loved Stella dearly, she felt as though she was with a very disapproving parent – whom she sometimes feared would reject her if she didn't behave.

Anna and Stella both felt positive and energised about becoming parents, but recognised that sometimes the roles that they undertook in their relationship could be getting in their way. Both of them explored what messages they each carried about parenthood from their own childhoods.

The Way Forward

Stella recognised that she'd internalised the complexity of her parents' marriage. On the one hand, keeping her emotions in the *background and hidden, and on the other hand, feeling compelled to support her partner no matter how she felt.*

Anna realised that she had cast Stella in the parental role. She wanted Stella to be like this so that she could continue to be taken care of as her mother had done. Anna also began to explore how she felt about not having a father figure growing up. She acknowledged that she felt rejected by this unknown figure, but also admitted that she never broached the subject with her mother for fear of hurting her feelings.

The counsellor questioned how Anna and Stella would themselves tackle these types of feelings with their own child. This enabled them to focus on what kind of parents they wanted to be.

The counsellor also worked with them on reframing their dynamic. They had to work out what their relationship was now, and to decide to both engage with their adult voices rather than continue the pattern of the parent–child dynamic. Stella's challenge was to stop seeing Anna as a naughty child who needed to be restrained, and Anna's challenge was to stop treating Stella like a parent by allowing herself to step into her adult self.

This helped them to start focusing on what kind of parents they wanted to be and on their next life-changing steps of starting their family.

PREPARING FOR LGBT PARENTING

Start off by asking yourself:

➤ What role do you play/does your partner play in your relationship?

➤ How will your lives change when you start a family?

➤ What role(s) do you want to undertake when a baby comes along?

➤ What role(s) do you expect your partner to undertake when a baby comes along?

Current circumstances:
- ➤ Do you as a couple have enough practical and emotional support around you?
- ➤ What is the strength and resilience of your relationship to handle going through a pregnancy, adoption, or fostering? See quiz on pages 151–5.
- ➤ Are you both on the same page about what you want? Again, see quiz on pages 151–5.
- ➤ Do either you or your partner want this more than the other?

Flash forward – you also need to consider the future:
- ➤ How do you imagine you will tackle tricky questions from your child such as: why do I have two mums/dads?
- ➤ How will you handle other people's assumptions/prejudices/curiosities/attitudes?

You will also need to think about what strategy you and your partner want to use in order to become parents. The options are adoption, being a foster parent, artificial insemination from a known or unknown donor, or choosing a male friend to inseminate or a female surrogate to carry your baby as appropriate. Each route will have its own pros and cons and it is important to sit down together and explore what would work best for both of you. This can feel overwhelming and I would recommend seeking advice in the first instance from an experienced counsellor to work through the psychological and practical aspects, and then legal advice – which will help you carefully think through the legal matters.

I know it may seem as though there are so many more factors to consider than your heterosexual counterparts, however, the more support, advice and information you have the better. Talk it out, discuss it, take advice and if you then decide that having children is for both of you – then go for it.

You are not alone, because there are a number of brilliant organisations who can help you through your journey – see Further Help on pages 271–4.

MISCARRIAGE

All the medical experts agree that a miscarriage is very common. The numbers vary slightly from one in three to one in five pregnancies. And even though it may be nature's way of telling us that something isn't quite right with the pregnancy it doesn't lessen the grief. It is very normal to experience grief for the baby that you did not meet, but carried for a while.

It is so important to get support during this time. When I had my miscarriage I was seven weeks pregnant, and in that time had welcomed the positive joy of becoming a mum into my world. I had already started to imagine what our lives would be like and how happy I was to be expecting my first child. The loss was shattering and I didn't want to talk to anyone except my partner at first.

Self-Help Tips: After a Miscarriage

1. It is important to acknowledge that the grief you feel is real no matter when in the pregnancy the miscarriage occurred. It is totally understandable to feel devastated – you had already begun to bond with your baby and form an emotional attachment.
2. Know that you are not to blame, it is not your fault and you certainly didn't do anything to deserve it.
3. Share your feelings with your partner rather than suffering in silence. You have both suffered a deep loss and your partner may be struggling with tough feelings too. Talking together will help both of you to heal.

4. If feelings become too hard to bear and your everyday functioning is affected – for instance if you're not sleeping properly or eating poorly, or feeling overwhelmed and tearful a lot of the time – then counselling might help you to release your feelings.
5. Support groups can be incredibly helpful if you want that, but don't feel you have to do this if you don't want to.

In time, the pain of the loss will end.

TRYING AGAIN

Deciding to try again for a baby will naturally bring up anxieties and that is why it is so important to allow yourself time to release sorrow from your loss. Getting pregnant may well bring about increased anxiety – this is a normal and natural reaction.

Give yourself permission to emotionally bond, rather than holding back for fear that something bad will happen. It's okay to have an array of mixed emotions; fear, joy, excitement – let them come through.

Look after yourself and engage in activities that give you pleasure. Spending time with friends, having a massage, gentle exercise, eating well. Choosing joyful and pleasurable activities will help you to reduce anxiety and distract you from negative thoughts.

———

Case Study: Losing Control

Dave (37) and Lesley (33) had been married for four years when Lesley became pregnant. Lesley's career in IT was blossoming and she had recently become head of two departments. Dave had been working as a fundraiser for a charity but had recently been made redundant. As a result of this, when Lesley became pregnant, they made the decision that Dave would become a house husband and be their child's main carer. Dave was more than happy with this and was looking forward to this next big challenge in their lives.

They were taken completely by surprise when at the 20-week scan, it was confirmed that they were having twins. They were both excited by the news, fully embraced the idea and had started to think about names for their babies.

Crunch Time

However, it was not long after this that Lesley miscarried. This was a massive shock to the couple and caused much grief, pain and feelings of guilt. Lesley blamed herself and had tremendous guilt and thought it was because she was working too hard. Dave described having his world totally blown apart.

For several months they struggled to come to terms with their loss. They couldn't fully comprehend what had happened and found it very difficult to share their depth of loss with each other. Lesley couldn't face talking to anyone about how she felt and as soon as she could she returned to work in the hope of everything going back to normal. She tried to be matter of fact about it, but found that she was on a short fuse and often very tearful. It was at this point that her boss suggested she take compassionate leave. Dave contacted the family doctor for advice and she recommended that they also have bereavement counselling.

Lesley

Lesley was the oldest of three girls and described having a very happy and structured childhood. Her parents, who were both in the medical profession, worked long hours but made a big effort to spend quality time with their children. She described them as positive, encouraging and wanting her to be the best. Lesley developed a real high-achievement approach to everything she did. As she got older, she recognised that she was often very competitive not only at work but in her personal relationships too. She almost always had to win arguments and found it hard to give in or apologise. Dave described her as his 'Little Type A'. She loved being in charge, which her sisters, past boyfriends and some friends found very difficult to be around after a while. Dave on the other hand, had a more laid-back approach and didn't mind her taking control. His niggles about her came from the fact that she was often very critical of him – she seemed to like pointing out his flaws. But no one was more critical of Lesley than Lesley herself. When she felt that she hadn't done something to the best of her ability, she would spend days painstakingly trying to figure out what she had done wrong. She described the loss of her twins as the saddest, most painful and biggest failure of her life.

Dave

Dave described having a carefree childhood. He had one younger brother who he was very close to and that bond had remained strong in his adult life. His mum was a freelance artist and his father was a woodcarver. He enjoyed the creative energy growing up, and Dave was encouraged from very early on to explore lots of things to find out what he enjoyed doing best. This freedom was a wonderful outlet for Dave, and he often hopped from one interest to the next without really taking anything up long-term. He had found school very difficult to settle into. He preferred to be outside exploring in the woods, rather than shut inside a room with other children. Dave's parents eventually pulled him out of school and he was home-educated, which he really loved. When Dave started working, he often chose short-term contracts that suited his style of working. He described finding institutions, structured environments and rules and regulations hard to deal with. When he met Lesley, he said that he'd finally found the person who complemented his nature. He was creative and free and she was organised and disciplined.

When Lesley miscarried, Dave described feeling overwhelming guilt that he had let her carry the burden of work and worry for the future while he'd just sat back and allowed this to happen.

The Way Forward

Lesley and Dave agreed to have some counselling sessions, but Lesley didn't feel that this would help her at all. As the sessions progressed, however, Lesley began to open up. Her sense of loss and feelings of failure were overwhelming. She sat and sobbed as if her heart would break. Dave felt helpless to support her and didn't know what to say.

The counsellor encouraged them to share their grief with one another because so far they'd been suffering alone. They described not wanting to burden each other, but soon realised that by staying away from each other's pain they'd felt their grief more intensely.

They admitted that not communicating difficult feelings was a familiar dynamic in their partnership. Lesley tended to be in charge, and Dave was often happy for her to take the lead. He described sometimes feeling inadequate living with his Little Type A. For him this meant being with someone who was always in control, could never switch off and have fun, and was always highly motivated to meet the next challenge. Lesley found this difficult to hear, but reluctantly agreed that without a sense of total control she felt very anxious. Both blamed themselves for the loss. Dave felt he could have done more to be supportive and Lesley felt that she'd put herself under undue pressure at work in order to ensure everything was in place before she went on maternity leave. Losing the babies for her meant losing total control, and she saw herself as a bad parent even before giving birth.

Sharing these difficult feelings was a big breakthrough for Lesley and Dave, and for several sessions the counsellor helped them to let go of the guilt and to focus on learning to communicate constructively and without criticism, blame or anger.

Lesley and Dave worked hard on this and both decided that they wanted a proper ritual where they could say goodbye to their babies. They had a naming ceremony with close friends and family and let one balloon go for each baby as a powerful symbol of saying goodbye and letting go. This cathartic exercise enabled them to emotionally move on.

They explored how they felt about becoming parents again and agreed to share how they were feeling – whether it was good, bad or scary – and vowed that they would support each other from now on.

They recognised that they could learn something from each other. Lesley agreed to take time off to allow her body and mind to recover and to learn to let go for a while. Dave recognised that this was his opportunity to contribute and take responsibility. He took up an offer of a one-year consultancy contract with a brand-new charity as their creative director. The job not only gave him a sense of control but also gave him a positive outlet too.

Six months after the counselling ended, Lesley discovered much to her delight that she was pregnant. She subsequently gave birth to a healthy baby daughter.

CHOOSING TO BE CHILD-FREE

Making a clear choice with your partner not to have children is a private and deeply personal decision. However, it often seems to bring out very vocal and emotional opinions in other people. The belief is that having a child is natural, so therefore choosing not to have one is perceived as unnatural. Some people do go as far as describing those who've chosen to be childless as selfish. The truth is that your decision may well bring out negative reactions from family, friends and even strangers. Whether it is parents who feel deprived of becoming grandparents or friends who stop inviting you to their home once they've started having their own children.

Being emotionally prepared as a couple for how to handle other people's reactions, as well as having a strategy to deal with any negativity, is the key to circumnavigating challenging situations and standing your ground.

Case Study: Just the Two of Us

Stuart (52) and Jenny (42) had been together for ten years. Stuart had recently taken early retirement from his job in the civil service and Jenny owned and ran her own hairdressing business. The two of them had met at a business networking event and they realised that they actually lived within a few miles of each other. They enjoyed each other's company and within a few weeks had started dating. Stuart had previously got divorced when he was 38, just at the time that his son had left home for university. He'd felt that his relationship had been rocky for a number of years, but he'd vowed to stay in it until his son was old enough to leave home.

When Stuart and Jenny moved in together, they had talked about the possibility of having a family. Stuart expressed that that phase of his life was over, but if Jenny seriously wanted a child of her own he would support her with that choice.

Since Jenny was in her twenties she had felt she wasn't the mothering kind. She liked children, but really couldn't imagine herself in that role. When her friends started to have children of their own she described herself as having a 'pang of motherhood' that very quickly faded. Jenny told Stuart very early on that she had no desire to have a family and was very happy with just the two of them. Jenny had also developed a strong bond with Stuart's son and his wife, and when they had their daughter, Lily, she was very happy to be part of Lily's life.

Crunch Time

Jenny had often felt the sting of criticism from friends because of her decision not to have children. She usually just shrugged this off. However, out for a stroll one day with her step-granddaughter, Lily, an old customer of Jenny's rushed up and congratulated her on finally giving in to nature and having her own baby. Jenny was taken aback and joked that she was actually the baby's grandmother. However, later on Jenny felt terrible. She told Stuart how other people's judgement of her was starting to get her down. She was beginning to feel growing pressure to do the 'right thing'. She questioned her own choices. She knew people thought she was selfish. However, she'd often stated how much more selfish it was to have a child if you didn't want one.

Jenny

Jenny had grown up in a large household with lots of brothers and sisters. She was the eldest of eight and often had to help her mother out with the younger siblings. By the time Jenny left home at 18 she was ready to start her own life, free of responsibilities to her family. When she was 24, her parents intimated that it was time for her to settle down, get married and start a family – after all, her mother had had her when she was 16. But Jenny told them that she'd not met the right person. She dated a lot of people, but never really wanted to do what her friends were doing – she often made it clear that she wasn't ready to settle for just anyone. When at 32 she met Stuart, she'd decided that having children wasn't for her and was very clear with him from the outset.

Stuart

Stuart described his family as very traditional. His dad worked and his mother looked after him and his younger brother. As a teenager he had lots of female friends and loved the attention he got from different girls. So, it was a surprise to everyone when at 19, he met a woman, fell in love and got married. By 20 he was a father. Stuart liked the security that having a family brought him, and he was a responsible and loving husband and father. His younger brother often teased him that he was old before his time.

As time went on, Stuart began to feel uneasy in his relationship and trapped by the responsibilities of marriage and fatherhood. He reacted by socialising regularly with colleagues after work, frequently coming home late and had had a couple of flirtations. He began to recognise that he'd gone head first into fatherhood and marriage without giving himself a chance to grow and develop as a person. At the same time, however, he had a long-held belief that loyalty and responsibility to your family came above your own desires. This was a message passed down from his own parents. He stayed with his wife until his son was old enough to leave home. He decided then that from now on he wouldn't rush into anything again and had learnt to voice his own needs and to be upfront about how he felt. This was one of the qualities that Jenny really appreciated about him.

The Way Forward

Jenny and Stuart recognised that there was a complexity of feelings about parenthood. He shared with her how he'd struggled with his own decision to put his son through a family divorce even though his son was an adult. He respected how Jenny had made her decision and stayed with it. Jenny shared how difficult it was to cope with other people's prejudices and critical judgements – that because she was a woman she should instinctively want to be a mother. Stuart said he sometimes wondered if Jenny would one day regret her choice.

By talking through their feelings about parenthood and their relationship priorities and choices, Jenny recognised that the pressure she was feeling was coming from other people's needs and not her own.

Stuart and Jenny stayed with their decision and made a pact to support each other – no matter what other people thought.

Self-Help Tips: Handling Others' Opinions when you're Child-Free

1. Your decision not to have children is strictly your business. Yes, other people are going to have opinions, but it is vital that you don't apologise for what you've decided to do.

2. It is important to check in with your partner and talk it out. How you are both feeling matters, especially when people can be negative towards you. This will really help strengthen your bond with each other.

3. It is normal to have doubts every now and again. You might be affected by your sister/close friends/neighbour having a baby and you may experience a pang of regret. Check in with yourself and see what this feeling may be telling you. If these feelings go away, then that's okay. If you find that it becomes a growing desire, then it could be that your feelings are changing and you may need to reconsider what you really want for yourself.

4. Practise excellent comebacks – and using humour can often work wonders. A friend of mine who was tired of endless questions about why she didn't want to have children took to wearing a T-shirt for a while that simply said, 'no kids, no problem'.

Becoming a parent is such a complex and lifelong decision for anybody and that decision deserves your time, your attention and your dedication. How you bond with your baby, express your love for them and nurture them, will influence them throughout their life. So it is so important that you as their primary care givers ensure that you and your partner are ready to give them love, structure and consistency.

But it is also important to ditch the idea of being perfect parents – I've spent years wanting to bump into them and have concluded that they don't really exist! Being a good enough parent is what truly matters. Your child won't fall apart if you occasionally get cross. However, they may feel neglected if you don't hug them often and tell them that you love them. Your child won't come to harm if you tell them off for covering the sofa in red paint. But they might come to harm if you push them away, abuse them or refuse to make time to cherish them and tell them how much they mean to you. Your child won't come to harm if you don't buy them the latest fashionable trainers, but they may suffer if you buy them expensive material things to compensate for your prolonged absence.

Being a parent *is* a very unique experience and can feel fulfilling, frustrating, scary, exciting, rewarding and challenging. In the next chapter, I'm going to look at the complexities of being in the step-parenting role and discuss how to handle the challenges that this can bring about.

Chapter 7
Blended Families

There used to be a very easily understood and narrow definition of what a family consisted of. Two parents and a couple of children made up the accepted description of the nuclear family. Not any more. The stepfamily or blended family is far more prevalent than ever before. And the number of blended families is growing.

According to statistics, blended families make up more than 10 per cent of all families in the UK, and research shows that because of the fact that the majority of children tend to stay with their mother following a divorce or separation, most blended families have a stepfather as opposed to a stepmother.[8]

I remember feeling too embarrassed to admit that I had a stepdad when I was at primary school, but by the time I was at university four out of five of the friends I house-shared with came from blended families.

I know first-hand from a child's eye how it feels to be in a blended family. A part of me was unhappy about it for years – until I learnt to: speak it, heal it and let go of it. My adult self has some sympathy with my stepfather (who is dead now) – he had never been a parent before and inherited a complex pre-teen. I was bereaved, scared, emotionally wounded and, yes, very angry. A few years earlier my parents had separated, ending their painfully miserable marriage, and not long afterwards my father died of a stroke. To make matters worse, my mother and I had to flee my birth country and so we came to England as refugees. Within a year my mother had married again. I became even angrier when my mother and stepfather created their own nuclear family by having their own child – and, as I saw it, excluded me. They could not quite find a positive space for me in the family and gave me the label of 'difficult child'. So, guess what? I lived up to my label. I refused point blank to take my step-father's surname, or call him 'Dad', and that was that!

It was only years later that I discovered that he too was brought up with a stepfather, and was told by his mother never to share this shameful secret with anyone. I had inherited an angry step-parent, who – perhaps with very little self-awareness – had acted out his angry and wounded younger self on to me. Having seen it from the other side as a therapist working with blended families, I've learnt to appreciate the complexity of emotions experienced by both children and their parents, as well as developing a deep understanding that with time, effort, commitment and plenty of patience, you *can* make it work.

A lot of clients have asked me how long it takes before things get easier or better within a blended family. I would love to give a definitive answer, a specific amount of time that they have to endure the emotional and practical challenges. The honest truth is that it depends, but as long as the parental figures are willing to work together positively then you will get there.

In this chapter I am going to take a step-by-step approach to handling the difficult situations you might face. It doesn't matter whether you are newly embarking on this journey or are several years into a blended family already, this chapter will help you work through the challenges and appreciate the rewards of being in a blended family.

There is no magic instant solution. However, how well you deal with the break-up of a relationship and manage relations with your ex, as well as create a workable framework for your children to handle the emotional and practical changes, sets the scene for what comes next. This can seem like a daunting task, and it isn't easy by any means. But the good news is that there are effective strategies that can help you handle the issues and successfully diffuse emotional bust-ups so that together you can all help to create and nurture a more loving environment.

I'm going to explore some of the complexities that occur at different relationship stages that may challenge you and bring into sharp focus your core beliefs about you as a person and you as a parent. If you already have children, the foundation within which you have been modelling relationships to them so far will also come into focus, as they also have to experience the daunting journey of living through uncertainty, insecurity and change. They will be reframing their own internal working model about how love and relationships work.

FAMILY BREAK-UPS

There is no doubt that the break-up of a relationship is distressing and difficult for all involved, even if separating is the best solution for everyone. There are emotional, practical and legal issues to tackle. There may be changes in standard of living if there's suddenly less money and there can be a move away from familiar surroundings. All these aspects are incredibly stressful for parents.

Stress may also see you and your existing partner behaving in negative ways. You might be experiencing intense angry feelings, guilt, anxiety about the future and worries about the children. Your default response to stress may click in and you may dig your heels in because you feel under threat, or perhaps you just want to run away from the pain of what is happening. Separation and divorce causes an emotional ripple effect, and family, friends and other relationships are touched by it. Their support or even lack of support will be informed by their own beliefs about love, marriage, separation and divorce, and will affect what they say to you and how they treat you.

THE EFFECT OF SEPARATING ON CHILDREN

Family breakdowns are very tough on children. Children like routine and structure and any changes to this can precipitate feelings of anxiety and fear. Children will let you know in their own way that they're distressed: from a drop in grades at school in a teenager, to bed-wetting, which can be a younger child's way of letting you know they are hurting by regressing to an earlier time. Depending on what age and development stage the children are, there will be different challenges and issues that will emerge.

Some experts suggest that the strongest predictor of a child being able to successfully cope with their parents' divorce is how well the parents get along. It isn't about pretending it's all hearts and flowers in front of the children: they would sniff out that kind of false behaviour immediately. It is more about parents having a relationship that is capable of basic communication for the sake of the children.

Children may have already coped with months or longer of a painful or even toxic atmosphere. They may have also witnessed too much, heard too much and felt extremely anxious and worried.

What children really want is routine, security and structure in their lives, and any change to this can bring about feelings of anxiety. When parents first split up their whole world is shaken and this can leave them feeling distressed, angry, sad, grieving or even lonely because suddenly everything feels very uncertain. Inevitably they also pick up on their parents' distress, and often witness and hear their parents going through the pain of the break-up. Psychologically, it takes time for a child to get over this and readjust to a new situation.

Now imagine those same children having to accommodate a parent's new partner into their lives. They may naturally feel hostile at first, trying to figure out how to fit in to this new relationship, and may see it as a threat. As a result they may jostle for attention, mark out their territory and act out all kinds of mixed emotions.

They will wonder if this new person is replacing Mum or Dad, and if not, who are they exactly in relation to them – friend, step-parent, Mum or Dad's new partner?

That's why it's vital to put your children's needs at the top of the priority list because creating a sense of stability and security is so important. The good news is that you can minimise their anxiety and pain by giving them practical and emotional tools to handle these challenging transitions.

———

Case Study: Tell Him to Go Away!

Marion and Jim

Marion (42) and Jim (50) had been separated for 18 months and were in the process of a divorce. They had three daughters, Lucy (23), Georgia (12) and Mimi (5). They had been married for 24 years and had got together romantically when Marion was 16 and Jim was 24. They came from a very close-knit community and their parents were very good friends with each other. People often described them as the perfect family: happy, sociable, outgoing with lots of support. Problems in the marriage began to emerge when Mimi, their youngest, was about 18 months old.

Marion

Marion was the youngest in her family, she had an older brother and sister. Her parents had split up when she was only six and over the years she had lost contact with her father. Her mother worked at the local council as an administrator and was proud of raising her children by herself. Marion had left school at 18 and decided to study for her vocational qualifications in hairdressing. She was passionate about hair and beauty and wanted to have her own salon eventually. She was just at the point of taking up a full-time trainee position at a health spa when Jim proposed. She was married and mum to Lucy by the time she was 19 and gave up on her dream. She loved being a mum, and Jim and Marion discussed having a big family. Jim enjoyed his family and liked his job as a supermarket assistant supervisor.

Marion had gradually been gaining weight over the years and felt very unhappy about the way she looked. Jim assured her that she looked beautiful to him and told her to stop worrying. Marion had also started to feel restless and felt that she was ready to go back into the workplace and resume her ambitions. She had, however, lost a lot of confidence and become withdrawn. When Lucy started at secondary school, Marion discovered that she was pregnant again. Jim was ecstatic and Marion, although delighted, felt resigned to the fact that she couldn't now work.

When Georgia entered Year 2 primary school, Marion became pregnant with Mimi and she decided that after this, she didn't want any more children.

Several months later, Marion was shocked to discover on a visit to the doctor that she had symptoms of prediabetes and she was advised to change her lifestyle and diet. Marion took this very seriously and asked Jim for support. He insisted that he liked her the way she was and she was worrying about nothing. This caused numerous rows and Marion felt very unsupported. But determined to get her health under control, she quit smoking, joined a weight-loss club and gradually started losing weight.

Within six months, Marion had lost weight, felt wonderful and had started working one and a half days a week at a local hairdressing salon. She thought Jim would be overjoyed for her. But during this time he'd become sulky and short-tempered. He said that pressures at work were getting him down and he complained that Marion was too busy to support him.

Jim blamed Marion's new lifestyle and said she never used to be this sassy before and he longed for her old self to return.

Marion started to feel guilty that she was being selfish and she couldn't take the arguments any more. She started to dread hearing his key in the door every evening.

Jim

Jim came from a very traditional background. Marion had often described him as her 'meat and potatoes man'. He was the youngest of three brothers and grew up with certain values about men and women. His father worked at the local brewery and his mother stayed at home to raise the family. Jim strongly believed that it was a man's job to support his family. And for Jim, as long as he was able to do this, he felt secure and happy.

When Marion started to change and gain her confidence back he felt very threatened, as though he no longer had a role to play as her husband. He didn't like what his wife was becoming and deep down feared that she would leave him. He often felt angry and defensive towards her, complaining that she was too thin now and he didn't fancy her any more. He refused to acknowledge that Marion was asserting herself and couldn't accommodate this psychological shift in power.

He'd never been happy that Marion was working, and the first time he'd really got angry was when she bought new living-room curtains with her own money. He responded by going out, getting drunk and ripping them off the curtain pole.

Jim's parents were very supportive of Marion because they knew what their son was like. Jim's mother recognised that she'd always done everything for her sons and Jim as the youngest was particularly spoilt. She blamed herself for his attitudes, but also felt somewhat helpless. Jim's father felt that his son's job was to support his family no matter what and was bitterly disappointed that Jim had shown weakness and failed in his marriage.

The Marriage Breakdown

Jim openly criticised Marion's weight, making fun of her and rubbishing her meals. The last straw for Marion came when Jim started trying to get the two youngest girls to agree with him. The children were being used as pawns in a power struggle and Marion could see it.

Marion wanted her and Jim to have counselling to sort out their problems, but he refused. He didn't want some stranger dictating to him what he should do in his marriage. Their marriage limped on for several months becoming more toxic. They'd stopped having sex and were barely speaking. Marion had finally had enough and she asked Jim to move out.

The separation was painful for all of them. Jim moved out of the family home and in with his parents. Marion and Jim barely communicated now unless it was about the children and their daughters had a difficult time trying to handle the changes. Georgia, who was particularly close to her dad, longed for him to move back home and often asked both her parents when this was going to happen.

For the sake of Georgia's feelings, Marion often responded to her daughter by saying that her and Jim were just having a rest from each other and they might get back together later. This promise was enough for Georgia to settle down for a while.

Marion and Tim

Marion met Tim (32) at the local gym where he'd just taken up his new post as the leisure centre manager.

Marion and Tim hit it off immediately and within a few months they'd started dating. She didn't want Tim to meet her children immediately and kept the relationship very low-key.

After several months, Marion began gradually introducing Tim as a friend. She'd taken the girls to the leisure centre for swimming sessions and they'd met him on neutral ground. Georgia was suspicious and a bit hostile, but Mimi was more at ease with her mum's new special friend. Once when Georgia saw her mum and Tim holding hands, she felt sick and burst into angry tears.

She refused to talk to her mum for a while, but confided in her older sister, Lucy. Lucy was very close to her mother and although she could see that her mother was struggling in the marriage at times, she still felt distressed by her parents' split. The breakdown in their marriage left her feeling anxious about her own relationship with her boyfriend, whom she'd just moved in with. Her core belief – that marriage equalled permanency – was now less certain and more fragile.

Crunch Time

Tim had been spending most weekends with Marion, sometimes at her place and sometimes at his, but never when the children were around. However, one weekend when Jim couldn't have the children, Marion decided that Tim could stay over. She'd planned for him to have left before the children woke up, but the girls got up early and went into their mum's room, as they often did for their morning cuddle. Georgia was horrified to find Tim in her parents' bed.

Georgia's behaviour changed. She felt very betrayed by her mother and very angry for being lied to. In her mind, Tim became a monster who was trying to ruin her family. Over several weeks, Georgia's behaviour deteriorated. She complained of stomach aches and didn't want to go to school. Her teachers noticed a drop in grades, but, worse still, her attitude had become defiant. Marion was called in for a meeting after Georgia had got into a fight with another girl. The school suggested the Georgia could talk to the school counsellor. Marion felt ashamed and embarrassed that she'd let her daughter down. She overheard a very distraught Georgia talking to Jim on the phone begging him to come back home.

Jim tried to be supportive while feeling furious that Marion had allowed another man into their home. He was angry that he'd lost his family and his wife. The separation from Marion had left him feeling powerless and emasculated.

The Way Forward

Jim realised that Georgia in particular was suffering. Georgia's schoolwork, her friendships and her health were being affected.

The shock of discovering his daughter's difficulties persuaded Jim to try mediation. Mimi was also beginning to show signs of distress. She'd been affected by Georgia's behaviour and found it hard to understand why Georgia attacked her for liking Tim.

He could see his children were suffering and, by him being so negative, they were getting worse. Marion admitted that not being crystal clear and honest with her daughters had left them feeling distressed and confused.

Mediation between Jim and Marion started off tentatively. There was still a lot of anger on both sides and both felt that they were the victim of the other's bad behaviour and for a while it felt to them as though they'd take two steps forward, only to take two steps back to square one. The mediator focused them on the key issue of how they wanted to move forward positively.

By taking a child-focused approach, Marion and Jim agreed to work together for the sake of helping their children handle the emotional transitions.

The Working Agreement
They agreed:

➤ *Not to criticise each other or talk negatively about each other in front of the children.*

➤ *They wouldn't use the kids to 'spy' on the other parent by probing them for information.*

➤ *They would keep each other informed if the children brought up any worries so that they could work together to support them.*

➤ *They would be open and honest with their daughters and take time out to speak to them individually.*

It was a slow process that required a lot of patience and at times it did break down, but Marion and Jim persevered and gradually things began to calm down. Georgia had some counselling sessions at school that helped her express how she felt in a safe space. The counsellor also helped her to use positive strategies to handle angry feelings. If Georgia felt too angry, she would write it all down and give it to her mum. This helped Marion and Georgia to start talking without tears and shouting. Over time, tensions eased and things gradually improved.

———

Self-Help Tips: Prioritising Your Children When Your Relationship Ends

1. **Reassure, reassure, reassure.** Your children need to know that even though you and your partner are separating, you are not divorcing them – they are still loved by both of you and are your number one priority. It is so important to reassure them that it is not their fault. Sometimes children do blame themselves and think it may be down to something they did, like that time that they did badly on a test or they got in trouble with a neighbour. And it is crucial to reassure them that it is not about taking sides. Repeat this message to them as many times as they need to hear it.

2. **Restraint in front of the children.** It can be difficult to hold back on angry feelings when emotions are running high and it can be difficult to compromise with someone whom you're feeling so angry with. But it is critical to be truthful with your children *without* pointing the finger of blame at each other. Make it a team effort when talking to the children. Agree what you are going to say to them about why you are separating. Be age appropriate. Don't go into long-winded explanations with young children – keep it simple. Older children may demand more detail, so give them what they need.

3. **Listen to them.** Children may not want to tell you how they feel at first. It is important that you encourage them to share how they feel and be prepared to listen to them. Sometimes they may not let you know how they feel in words, but with behaviour, so pick up on their moods. You may want nothing more than to magic away their

pain and see them smile again, but acknowledging that they're sad is important. That way, they know that they can be honest with you, rather than swallow down painful feelings and hide them from you.

4. **Provide structure and routine.** It is vital to create space to have time-limited, battle-free conversations that focus on arranging specifics for the children. You should keep it centred on the children – this will help both of you focus on what matters. Things you will need to discuss are:

> ➤ What needs organising for the sake of the children.
> ➤ Arranging an agreed timetable.
> ➤ Organising childcare arrangements.
> ➤ Who is going to look after the children on specific days and times.

Then tell the children exactly how their new routine is going to work. Be clear and honest about the fact that some things will be the same and some things will change.

All these arrangements will give your children a sense of certainty about what is happening and when. This can really help both younger and older children deal with the difficult changes and give them a sense of order and stability.

5. **Kids not spies.** Tempting as it may be, don't use your children as a go-between to find out what your partner is up to; whether it is that you suspect your ex may be seeing someone else or as a way to find out about finances. These are no-go areas to discuss with your children. It confuses them, makes them feel like they have to choose sides and leaves them feeling emotionally trapped.

The Long View
Sometimes having to battle with your ex-partner can leave you wondering why you're bothering. But imagine how you'd

like your children to be in five or ten years from now in terms of their resilience and emotional well-being. They'll be influenced by their experiences. Seeing their parents handle difficulties in a constructive way will equip them to deal with challenges that may occur in their own lives and enable them to form healthy attachments. Keeping this thought in mind can help you handle small niggles and ditch petty battles.

Serious Concerns

It is totally normal for children to feel angry and sad some days, anxious on other days and sometimes to say they feel fine. Some children may feel a sense of powerlessness and seem a bit helpless at times, which could signal a mild form of depression. It can feel awful to witness your children feel like this, but with time, your loving support and perseverance they should slowly improve. However, if you notice that after several months your children are worse and showing little or no sign of feeling better, then they may be exhibiting signs of prolonged emotional distress.

Let your child's school know what the family are going through and ask them to keep you informed of any changes in your child's behaviour. Some schools do have access to school counsellors and this may help your child to talk through their own feelings in a safe space. This can really help children if they feel as if they're stuck in the middle or as though they have to take sides.

Red Alerts

This list is by no means exhaustive, but more an indication for what to look out for:

➤ Poor concentration.
➤ A drop in grades at school.
➤ Complaining of stomach aches and not wanting to go to school.

➤ Frequent angry outbursts.
➤ Becoming clingy.
➤ Withdrawal behaviour (a normally outgoing child who chooses to isolate themselves, spends a lot of time alone and distances themselves from their friends).
➤ Reckless behaviour (such as drinking, smoking and drug taking).

Take these indicators seriously and act quickly. Discuss them with your child's teacher, GP or a counsellor who specialises in working with children as it's important to get extra support.

ABOUT YOU

You need to look after yourself. Separation and divorce may be the best thing to do, but it still takes its toll emotionally and physically. One client described it to me as 'the cruellest living loss' that left her drained physically and spiritually.

Make sure you have plenty of support from family and close friends. Professional support at a time like this can be beneficial too so that you have a safe place to express your feelings.

Don't be afraid to lean on friends. If you need their support, whether it's picking the children up or just sitting down and having a heart to heart, then do it. Isolation, bottling feelings up and suffering alone will make you feel worse.

Get rest, eat well and allow yourself time out to look after your needs. Whether it is going to get your hair done, doing some exercise or getting a massage. Your well-being matters.

COMMUNICATION BREAKDOWNS WITH EXTENDED FAMILY MEMBERS

When a couple breaks up, the emotional ripple effect is far-reaching, from children, parents and in-laws to friendships and even work colleagues.

Whatever the reason for the relationship ending, communication breakdowns do happen as a result. It may be angry in-laws who blame you for the break-up of the relationship and so refuse to speak to you, or a jealous ex-partner who may stop communicating properly and become obstructive because you've met someone else.

In these trying circumstances it is vital to acknowledge difficult feelings, but to maintain the emotional and practical needs of the children as top priority. This can help keep you focused at times when negative feelings can be overwhelming.

———

Case Study: There Are Too Many of Us in this Relationship

Chris (49) and Joyce (38) had been living together for the last year. They'd met at a family holiday resort in Spain during the school summer break and quickly found out that they had quite a lot in common and actually didn't live that far away from each other back home. Joyce was on holiday with her two sons David and Matthew, who at the time were nine and seven. Two years earlier, her husband Michael had died suddenly of a stroke when he was 44. This was Joyce's first holiday abroad with her sons after their family bereavement. It had taken a lot for her to find the strength and confidence to get out into the world again, but she could see that her sons needed some fun back in their lives after such a deep loss.

Chris was on holiday with his daughter, Izzy. He was divorced from his wife Dee-Dee after 15 years of marriage. Dee-Dee and Chris had a joint residency agreement and had arranged that every summer holiday Izzy would spend three weeks with her dad. This was their second summer holiday together.

Joyce and Chris got talking while waiting to pick their children up from the activities club. They arranged to meet later on with the kids for a meal. Over the course of the holiday, both of them opened up about their personal circumstances. Joyce found it so refreshing that

Chris allowed her to talk freely about her husband and allowed her the space to express how she felt. Most of her close friends were still treading on eggshells to avoid upsetting her. Chris talked about his ex-wife and how they'd grown apart over the last five years. Chris shared that his ex had had a brief fling shortly after he'd been made redundant from the construction company where he worked. He'd found it incredibly hard to deal with, but the marriage struggled on for several months. They'd stopped talking, slept in separate rooms and started to drift apart. Chris couldn't tolerate things the way they were any more and filed for divorce.

Joyce and Michael

Joyce and Michael were happily married for 10 years. They met through mutual friends when Joyce was 25 and Michael was 34. They had two sons whom they absolutely adored. Michael was deputy head at the local comprehensive and Joyce worked part-time at the primary school that her sons attended. They were a happy family, had a lot of friends and were very involved in their local community.

However, Michael was taken very ill at work one day and within hours he'd died of a stroke. This was a terrible shock to the family and left Joyce in pieces. It took several months for her and the boys to comprehend their sudden and shocking loss.

Joyce felt that she suddenly had to become mum and dad to her children. From clearly knowing what her role was in her marriage to Michael, she suddenly had to become aware of everything. Michael had always done the paperwork and although he had left a will and most of the paperwork was in good order, Joyce felt nervous about taking full control. She realised that she'd often taken a backseat; even when Michael used to try to involve her and explain the finances to her, she would often just switch off.

But gradually, over time, they began to rebuild some kind of life without Michael. Joyce had a lot of family support, as well as some bereavement counselling to try to come to terms with their loss. David was very badly affected and it took some time before he could open up about his dad. He was very close to his dad and carried some guilt that on the day his dad died he hadn't got up early enough to give his dad his usual hug goodbye.

Michael's mother, Tina, had been widowed four years earlier and was deeply shocked by the loss of her only son. Joyce and Tina became very close during this period and spent a lot of time consoling and drawing strength from each other. Tina had become very isolated after her husband's death and had few friends, whom she seldom saw. When Michael was alive, they used to see Tina as a family only about twice a month because of their schedules and busy lives. As she grew closer to Joyce and the boys, she became a much more regular part of their lives and began to feel that she had an important role to play; she felt needed.

When Joyce shared with Tina that she'd met Chris and was beginning to have feelings for him, Tina became very upset and started to say very negative things about Chris in front of the children. Deep down she feared that she'd be rejected and left out of their family completely if Chris and Joyce's relationship became more serious.

Chris and Dee-Dee

Chris had been divorced from his wife Dee-Dee for two years and had a daughter, Izzy, now aged 11. Chris's work ethic and driving ambition had caused major problems early on in their relationship.

They had several financial problems because Chris overstretched himself to provide Dee-Dee with every material comfort. She had complained that Chris was hardly ever at home to help her with Izzy. What Dee-Dee really wanted from Chris was closeness and reassurance that everything would be all right. She often felt insecure about how he really felt about her and this sometimes caused her to be critical and negative towards him. Chris thought he was reassuring her by trying to provide her with the material comfort she desired. It was his way of showing her love. He often felt uncomfortable communicating his true feelings and anxieties – and although he wanted to let Dee-Dee in, he felt safer keeping her at an emotional distance. Chris had ambitions for his daughter and enrolled her at an expensive prep school, stating that it was the best school in the area, which meant he had to work longer hours to fund it.

When Chris started to hear rumblings at work that there were going to be possible redundancies made, he was worried that as one of the highest-paid managers he could be targeted. However, he hid these fears from Dee-Dee. For several weeks, while Chris waited for a decision, their relationship deteriorated. He didn't tell her what was really going on, but instead got angry with her, at what he saw as her wasting money on frivolous things. He became furious when Dee-Dee suggested that if he was worried about money, then they should at least consider putting Izzy into the local primary school. He refused, arguing that he wanted the best for his daughter. For the sake of keeping things together, Dee-Dee gave in and kept quiet.

Over time, Dee-Dee started talking to one of the dads at Izzy's school about how unhappy she was. It was this man with whom she had a brief fling, shortly after Chris lost his job. She knew she'd made a mistake and confessed straight away to Chris. She also told him that she felt their lives were spiralling out of control because he wouldn't share his feelings with her.

Chris was very bitter and he felt that Dee-Dee had kicked him when he was down. Both of them wanted to try to salvage the relationship for the sake of their daughter and tried counselling, but Chris couldn't get past his anger about Dee-Dee's betrayal and so filed for divorce.

Chris and Joyce

Chris and Joyce started seeing each other at first as friends and a source of mutual support. However, after a while, their relationship became deeper – they both felt that they had connected on a much more profound level. They had talked about consolidating their lives and moving in together, but Joyce had been reluctant to upset her sons' routines. They'd begun to settle down into a different pattern of life and Joyce recognised that keeping things constant, familiar and safe was helping them to start healing.

Izzy had her routine where she spent three and a half days a week with Chris and the rest of the week with her mum. Dee-Dee had wanted out of the family home and she and Izzy had moved into a flat nearby that Chris paid the rent on, while Chris remained in the house.

Izzy got on with Joyce and mostly tolerated Matthew and David, although she didn't like it when she heard about her dad spending time with them when she wasn't there. She sometimes felt as though she was being replaced by them.

However, due to increasing financial pressures on Chris, he finally agreed that he and Dee-Dee would sell the family home. Once the house was sold, Joyce suggested that Chris move in with her as a temporary measure to save him the hassle of renting while looking for somewhere else to live. She suggested that this could also be a good litmus test to see if living together would work or not.

At first things were okay, Joyce explained to her sons that this would just be for a short while until Chris found another place to live. They were both hopeful that the children would be all right with this, because the children were of similar ages. After a few months, Chris and Joyce decided that the arrangement was working well and made the decision to make it more permanent.

The children were okay at first because it felt like a bit of an adventure, but once the honeymoon period was over and the reality set in that this was how it was going to be from now on, issues started to arise.

Crunch Time

Dee-Dee was incredibly unhappy about her daughter moving in for half the week with another family. She was livid that she hadn't been consulted properly and felt that she'd been led to believe that this was a temporary measure. She felt strongly that Izzy was no longer Chris's priority.

Izzy felt that she had no space at Joyce's house and was stuck in a little box room. Chris felt guilty about this and overcompensated by constantly lavishing her with expensive gifts.

Joyce felt that Chris was very hands-off with boundaries whenever Izzy came to stay. She was allowed to stay up late on school nights, which caused problems with her sons who complained that this wasn't fair.

David got upset if Matthew sometimes sat on Chris's lap to have a story read to him and would sometimes come and push Matthew off, making it very clear that this was not their dad. If Chris told the boys off for something, David's angry reaction was often, 'You're not my dad and you can't tell me off.'

Chris and Joyce hadn't discussed their joint finances and this became an area of unspoken contention. Chris still had a few financial debts, but continued to pay for Izzy's private education. Joyce thought this was a waste of money, but didn't feel able to bring this up with Chris so she let it go.

Izzy became fearful that her presence was causing problems for her dad and Joyce and she decided that, even though she loved her dad, maybe it was best to live with her mum full-time.

The Way Forward
Chris and Joyce were feeling overwhelmed emotionally, as if they were being pulled in so many different directions all at once and their own relationship was being torn apart. Joyce felt that the key to resolving a lot of the difficulties was for the three parents to sit down and sort things out.

Chris
Chris's pattern of behaviour had always been to bury himself in work and not face up to problems. In the past, whenever Dee-Dee was upset he'd often respond by showering her with gifts. He was beginning to repeat the pattern with his daughter and it was affecting his relationship with Joyce. Chris had a strongly held belief that it was his job to provide for his family at any cost – and this is how he'd learnt to show love. He also found it difficult to admit to problems and believed in self-reliance rather than sharing problems with his partner.

Joyce

In her previous marriage, Joyce had deferred to Michael on the big decisions – from where to live, to what school their children attended. She liked the security of someone taking care of her and the family. The loss of Michael had forced her to take control of everything and she was beginning to feel more self-empowered. However, she admitted that inviting Chris to move in so soon was also driven by her need for the security of a relationship. She was beginning to notice that her need for security sometimes meant that she didn't speak up and challenge Chris with things that she just didn't agree with. This was now not only affecting her, but her children as well.

Dee-Dee

Dee-Dee was devastated by the end of her marriage to Chris. Although she'd finally accepted that the marriage was over, and was herself seeing someone else on a casual basis, she was angry to find out that he'd moved into another relationship so quickly, and felt a pang of jealousy. As a result, she'd been using Izzy to find out information about Joyce, her home and her sons. This had left Izzy feeling very torn between her parents.

Joyce and Chris finally sat down together and put their individual and joint concerns on paper. They discussed what needed to happen in order for things to run smoother for the sake of the children and for their relationship. Chris agreed that it was crucial that all the children should see that the parents were being civil to each other in the first instance.

They then sat down with the children and asked them what they'd like to happen.

The strongest message from Izzy was that she desperately wanted her parents to get on. Izzy also felt that when she was at Joyce's house she didn't belong and she felt like the outsider. She hated feeling like this.

Matthew didn't really mind Chris, but felt that he had to follow his brother and behave badly towards him sometimes. David really *disliked Chris because he thought Chris was trying to replace his dad. He also felt deep down that even starting to try to like Chris a tiny bit meant that he was betraying his dad. The boys asked for time alone with their mum and to not have to call Chris 'Dad'.*

Dee-Dee agreed to meet with Joyce and Chris for the sake of her daughter, and they agreed together on what was okay and not okay for Izzy. Chris and Dee-Dee would go to all Izzy's school events together so that she had her parents there.

Joyce and Chris would help Izzy create a space in their home that made Izzy feel welcome and part of the family.

Chris, however, refused for now to budge on Izzy's schooling and wanted his daughter to stay at her school for the foreseeable future. He agreed to stop buying her expensive gifts to appease her and instead to create special time with her on her own so that she didn't feel emotionally neglected.

Over time, Joyce tentatively introduced Chris to Tina and worked towards making her still feel that she was part of the family. She also arranged for Tina to have the boys for a couple of hours once a fortnight so that they had their own special time with their nan.

———

CHANGING ROLES

Whether you are thinking of merging two families together or there is one new partner about to enter an existing family, you are going to experience a myriad of conflicting and painful emotions. First off, you already had established roles and routines within the primary family that everyone understood. These then come to an end, either abruptly or slowly and painfully, whether through bereavement, separation or divorce.

Then you meet someone new. You fall in love and you decide to merge your lives. If they also have children they'll have their own routine, rules and established ways of operating with the kids. If either party doesn't have children they'll still have their own routine and ways of behaving with the different children who enter their lives.

Therefore you have to go back to the beginning, establishing new rules and routines for your own children, as well as potentially trying to establish and build an attachment with someone else's children, while at the same time trying to create and maintain a loving dynamic with your new partner. Roles may get confused – are you parent or friend to your stepchildren? Do your partner's rules and style of parenting match yours? Are your children used to strict discipline while your partner's children enjoy a more laissez-faire approach?

This is all before you even consider how you are going to manage the relationship with the ex, or deal with constant comparisons with an idolised parent who passed away, or handle resentments from children who hope their parents will get back together again – and so see you as the hostile enemy.

Self-Help Tips: Blended Families

1. It's vital not to force your children to like your partner. They already have a lot to deal with and they need time to get used to a new set of circumstances. Give them space and time to come to terms with it.

2. Within your blended family it is important to make time for your own children. They may start to feel that they are not priority or don't matter to you as much as they used to. Having special time with you can help them to feel secure and loved. Whether it's making time every Saturday to watch them at their football game or going to the cinema together, make sure you create that special bonding time.

3. If you and your partner have a baby within your new family, it is very important that your other children don't feel as though they are being replaced. They may well experience feelings of anxiety about this. Yes, your new

baby is important and a symbol of your union, but the other children need to feel as though they're an integral part of the family.

4. When it comes to discipline things can get tricky and, honestly, a bit messy. Start by agreeing house rules that all the children have to keep to and then make sure you follow through. Don't try to take over the parenting if you're in the step-parenting role – this will cause major tensions. It is important to present a united front, a united set of family rules and to back up your partner, but trying to place your stamp of authority over your stepchildren while the birth parent takes a back seat may lead to dissent.

5. As the birth parent of your children it is important that they don't see you hand over control to their step-parent. This may leave them feeling as though you can't and don't want to deal with them any more.

There are multiple feelings, challenges and practicalities to deal with when considering binding different lives and family members together. However, keeping children as the central focus can help to give you an excellent starting point in order to work out what needs to be agreed on and where compromises may need to be made. This will help you to manage tricky relationship challenges and ensure that your children are better able to survive, handle and move on from the pain of divorce, separation or bereavement.

Chapter 8
Surviving Crises and Learning to Manage the Bumps in the Road

No matter who you are or how stable or happy your relationship seems to be, no one is immune from crises. Whether it's a midlife crisis fuelled by feelings that you're running out of time to achieve all your ambitions or feeling life is passing you by, to illness, bereavement, infertility, career change or in-laws causing tensions. One minute you're minding your own business, happy enough in your relationship and life is on an even keel, when circumstances change that test you and your partner to your limits. Add to this the likelihood that you and your partner react differently to the same set of circumstances and you may find that you're pulling in opposing directions.

Of course you can't prepare for or control every eventuality – because things do happen that throw you out of your comfort zone. But in this chapter I'm going to focus on a step-by-step approach to *managing* adversity. I will include positive and effective self-help strategies to help you develop a constructive approach, so that you can successfully circumnavigate the tough times together, no matter what life throws at you.

CORE BELIEFS

Your core beliefs can affect your ability to be resilient during the tough times. How you see yourself can affect how you approach challenges, adversity and failure. Imagine how a person whose core belief about themselves is that they are always 'in control'. Their ability to handle circumstances where they have absolutely no control would test them to the limit. They may then choose to dig their heels in and be in denial about not having control, resulting in their inability to behave flexibly. Of course this reaction would have a knock-on effect on their relationship too.

The good news is that understanding how you behave as a couple when the chips are down is a crucial first step. This means that not only are you self-aware, but are also open to learning and integrating effective ways to deal with adversity in a more manageable and realistic way, so that when bad stuff happens, you can handle it.

MANAGING ADVERSITY: YOUR RELATIONSHIP STRENGTHS AND CHALLENGES

Your relationship may have already experienced and survived a number of ups and downs. It is important to take stock of how well or not you as a couple have handled the challenges so far.

This quick quiz is for both of you to do and will help you to:

1. Examine what role you play in your relationship when faced with adversity, and
2. Identify the strengths and weaknesses of your relationship when things go wrong.

Consider these statements and answer on a scale of 1–5.
1 = strongly agree, 5 = strongly disagree.

1. About me. When things go wrong, I tend to:
➤ Feel helpless.
➤ Take control.
➤ Look for someone to blame.
➤ Roll my sleeves up and get on with it.
➤ Enjoy the challenge.
➤ Look to my partner to take over.

2. About us. How supportive you are of each other during the good and the tough times is important to assess. This way you can evaluate whether your relationship support is out of balance or not, and will recognise where strengths and weaknesses lie.
➤ We don't always agree, but we say sorry to each other if we see that we were hurting each other's feelings.
➤ I know, deep down, that if I was struggling with something my partner would do all they could to support me.
➤ My partner has always been my greatest supporter.
➤ I can trust that my partner would never bad-mouth me behind my back.
➤ My partner and I are able to tell each other what we need/want from one another.
➤ My partner tends to blame me when things do go wrong.
➤ When my partner makes a mistake I spend weeks bringing it up and blaming them.
➤ I feel so angry when my partner makes a mistake.

➤ I feel helpless when things go wrong and turn to my partner to sort everything out.

➤ My partner almost always leaves me to sort out our problems.

➤ My partner hardly ever sticks up for me.

➤ I hardly ever stick up for my partner.

➤ We as a couple have a tendency to act as individuals and pull in different directions.

➤ We as a couple have a tendency to let small problems grow into bigger crises.

➤ We as a couple tend to work together as a team.

➤ Past problems have weakened our relationship.

➤ Past problems have made us stronger than ever.

Use this quiz as a positive communication tool and share your answers with each other. This will help you to identify where your relationship strengths and weaknesses lie.

It is during crises when weaknesses manifest themselves and are brought to your attention, usually in the most emotionally raw way – whether it's angry outbursts, blaming, sulking, fearing or hiding. That's why it becomes vital in your relationship to know where your vulnerabilities lie so that you can recognise them and understand how to strengthen them.

Having done the quiz and shared your responses, you may find that you have already developed an effective and constructive way of handling problems. If, on the whole, you and your partner are supportive of one another, tend to be a united front and work as a team and don't spend a lot of time pointing the finger and blaming each other, then that's brilliant. You have a healthy strategy for handling adversity.

If, however, you discover that your default setting is to lean more towards blaming each other and pulling in different directions, then the good news is that being able to recognise that this is what you do is the first step to changing it.

AVOIDING NEGATIVE PATTERNS

Sometimes as a couple you can both get stuck in habitual negative ways of behaving without consciously being aware of what you are doing. This way of behaving has become so well practised over time that it becomes part of your relationship default setting, you're both so used to it that it seems automatic. Whether it is handling the in-laws or both playing the blame game (where your partner blames you and you immediately blame back), or covering up for bad behaviour (if your partner's habitual lateness to social events leaves you feeling embarrassed but you continue to make excuses for them to friends and family). You know that these behaviours are hurting both of you, but feel stuck and unsure of how to change things for the better.

I'm going to deal with some key events that often come up that reflect unhelpful patterns of behaviour that sometimes emerge when crises happen. These examples are to demonstrate and highlight how to break negative patterns of behaviour and replace them with workable and realistic solutions to help you get through the tough times.

COPING WITH THE IN-LAWS

Whether you are married or in a long-term, committed relationship, you and your partner cannot detach yourselves from the rest of your family. You come as a package, whether the relationship with the rest of the family is good, bad or indifferent. Some in-laws operate as though their child is an extension of themselves and as a result may behave in ways that are intrusive, unboundaried or judgemental (as we have seen in Chapter 5). For others, the relationship with the in-laws might be fairly easy at first, where you fit in with their dynamic and they adore you, until something happens that destabilises the relationship.

Shifts in the relationship's power balance may arise over issues such as your wedding – from who is paying, who to invite, who to leave out, to where the ceremony will be held. The birth of your first baby could see the once harmonious relationship with your in-laws turn into a battleground over who knows best for the baby, or your in-laws might demand that your partner spends more time with them because they have priority over you!

Your in-laws haven't chosen you and you haven't chosen them, but you all have to get along for the sake of the one person you all share in common. Experiencing tensions, a tug of love and power struggles can so easily happen when you are in a triangular relationship like this.

Like any relationship it takes time, compromise, commitment and mutual respect to make it work. But again, like any relationship, you may get caught up in emotions running high, playing out old scripts and clashing on differing beliefs and values, which can lead to relationships getting stuck or worse still, breaking down completely.

———

Case Study: Stop Intruding

Phoebe (32) and Sean (38) had been together for six years. They were married and had a son, Patrick (2). Sean worked in hotel management and Phoebe was a PE teacher.

They'd met in an airport lounge when their flight to Australia had been delayed for several hours. Phoebe was on her way to visit her sister and Sean was off on holiday with a group of friends.

Sean had been watching Phoebe as she paced impatiently up and down, occasionally accosting airport staff and giving them a piece of her mind about the flight delay. They got talking and enjoyed each other's company. Phoebe loved that Sean calmed her down by making her laugh and that she felt at ease in his company.

After a few months of texting, they finally met up again and decided that there was more to their meeting than just social flirting. Within two years they'd moved in together and were married.

Phoebe and Sean had a happy and vibrant relationship most of the time. They were planning to start a family soon and in the meantime were enjoying their time together as a couple.

Phoebe recognised that she gave Sean permission to express himself. He shared with her how she'd influenced him positively to speak his mind and be more emotionally open. Sean told her that he was attracted to her strength and can-do attitude, and he felt safe with her. Being with Phoebe, Sean had become more emotionally assertive and boundaried – except in his relationship with his mother.

Over time, the issue of Sean's mother Heather began to emerge more clearly. Phoebe had had a long-running gripe about how Heather, who lived alone, seemed to demand so much of his free time. This pattern had been set up long before Phoebe had ever met Sean and it was something that Sean felt unable to change. At the beginning of December each year, almost like clockwork, Sean would get a phone call from his mother telling him that she was suffering from palpitations and couldn't come to visit him at Christmas, and asking him to go and stay with her instead. Phoebe at first tolerated this out of concern that Sean's mother was unwell. But this often meant that Phoebe and Sean were either together at Christmas with Heather or that they spent Christmas apart with their respective parents.

Heather's behaviour wasn't confined to Christmas. Whenever she felt anxious or left out of Sean's life she would phone him in floods of tears, complaining of chest pains. This could be in the middle of the night, the start of a weekend or when she knew that Sean and Phoebe would be preparing to leave for a holiday. Her phone calls would have Sean panicking, jumping into his car and racing to her side.

Heather had been divorced from Sean's father for 20 years and she'd had several intense relationships that didn't last very long. Her dates had noted that after being charming at first, she'd soon become clingy and demanding. She had a similar pattern in friendships.

Phoebe and Sean had a few disagreements about Heather's behaviour. Phoebe was concerned that Sean was getting unnecessarily stressed out by his mother and accused Heather of just putting it on. This would trigger Sean into uncharacteristic anger and he'd become very defensive about his mother.

When Heather discovered that she was going to become a grandmother, she was excited at first, but then the number of times she contacted Sean saying that she was ill increased.

Once Sean and Phoebe's son was born, things between Phoebe and Heather got a lot worse. Phoebe had been very resentful that Heather had turned up late to the hospital the day Patrick was born. Heather had apologised profusely saying that it had taken two hours for her to find parking, however, Phoebe just saw this as another example of her drawing attention to herself.

When Heather visited them she started to become very critical of Phoebe's parenting skills. She had never been particularly warm towards Phoebe, but had politely tolerated her. Now, she complained to Sean that Phoebe was holding the baby all wrong, claiming that, as an ex-social worker who worked in child protection, she knew what was best for their son. She started bossing Phoebe about, criticising the way she was feeding Patrick and telling her that even considering going back to work meant that she was selfish and not putting the needs of her child first.

Phoebe was often left in floods of frustrated tears after Heather's visits. She confided in her own parents and her mother advised her to speak to Sean before things got out of hand.

Phoebe and Sean finally sat down to talk. She started off by telling him how much she loved him and Patrick – they had a lovely life together, but that she felt crushed by Heather's criticisms. Sean knew that his mother was being awful to Phoebe and he *promised to talk to her. Phoebe didn't feel confident that he'd actually do it.*

Sean

Sean was brought up an only child and was very close to both his parents. His father worked as a vet and Sean often spent quite a lot of time with him when he was young and had wanted to follow in his footsteps. His mother worked part-time as a social worker and was an active and popular member of the community.

Sean remembers his mother being the more vocal and domineering parent. Whenever Heather would get angry or upset, Sean's father simply wouldn't engage and would just leave the room. After one particularly terrible row between his parents, his father threatened to leave if she continued to put him down and undermine him in public. Shortly afterwards, Sean remembers his mother being taken into hospital with what was at first thought to be a suspected heart attack (it was in fact an anxiety attack). Sean was about seven years old when this happened and this frightening event was seared into his memory. He still carried around the emotions with him many years later. His parents' marriage struggled on for years in this cycle of behaviour. Each time his father spoke up for himself, his mother would get sick.

Sean's father eventually ended the marriage when Sean was old enough to go to college. He maintained contact with Sean and Phoebe and asked them early on in their relationship that as much as possible they should organise to see him and Heather separately.

Sean loved spending time with Phoebe's parents. They were open and honest with each other and, even after all this time together, had a lively and loving relationship. They didn't always agree with each other, but somehow managed to talk things out without descending into a negative drama cycle. This is what he wanted his own family to be like.

Sean recognised that in some ways he'd picked up where his father had left off and was enabling his mother to play out her very familiar old script. He could see on the one hand that his mother tended to manipulate people in order to keep them close, but on the other hand, part of him still feared that maybe she really was ill and he'd never forgive himself if something bad did happen to her.

Sean's father could see how his son was feeling and told him not to be manipulated. The difficulty for Sean was that whenever he spoke to his mother about Phoebe, she would apologise and be very remorseful, and then would be utterly charming and loving for weeks. Then, just when things were going well, she'd start picking on Phoebe again.

Phoebe

Phoebe was the youngest of two sisters and her parents had been married for 35 years. Her family were originally from Leeds, but had moved to Australia before their children were born and lived there until Phoebe was 16. Phoebe experienced her family culture as very straight-talking and outspoken. The girls grew up to be confident, strong and outgoing. Phoebe's parents had owned a farm for many years, before moving back to the UK. Their oldest daughter remained in Australia with her own family.

Crunch Time

It was during one of Heather's more charming phases that Phoebe and Sean agreed that she could babysit Patrick. They went round to her house, had lunch with her and agreed that they'd pick Patrick up a couple of hours later. Patrick was two years old at this point and very active and lively.

Heather seemed happy to have the opportunity to spend time on her own with her grandson. Phoebe was a little nervous, as she knew Heather was unpredictable at times and didn't quite trust her. However, for Sean's sake, she decided not to say anything. Sean was hopeful all would be okay.

However, as they were getting ready to leave, Heather said to Patrick, 'Grandma makes nicer food than Mummy's – hers is yucky.' Sean quietly picked up his son and told his mother that she'd finally gone too far and that he'd no longer tolerate her vicious comments against his wife – especially in front of his son. They left Heather's house, got in the car and drove back home.

When Phoebe told her mother, Debbie, of the incident, she was so angered that she phoned Heather and ended up rowing with her. This made matters worse and caused rows between Phoebe and Sean.

For weeks, Heather didn't contact Sean, which made him feel helpless. Phoebe could see that Sean was struggling and that it had taken an awful lot of strength for him to stand up to his mother. Sean acknowledged that it had taken him a long time to speak up and he knew that Phoebe had felt betrayed by his silence.

The Way Forward

They tried to figure out what to do. Sean knew that he couldn't just cut his mother out of his life and felt that it was important for Patrick to have a relationship with her. Phoebe felt that this was his decision to make, even though deep down she saw Heather as controlling and chaotic whenever it suited her. She didn't want her own son to be influenced by someone with such messy and unpredictable feelings.

Sean contacted Heather and had an honest discussion with her. He told her that, although he wanted her in his family's life, she had to stop behaving in a way that was harmful to all of them. He was shocked when he realised that Heather wanted him to put her needs before his own wife's needs and that she felt betrayed when he didn't automatically defend her against Phoebe. It was this faulty belief that was fuelling her anger, and Sean felt as though he had effectively been cast in the role of surrogate husband by his own mother.

Sean decided it was time to put firm boundaries down and was finally clear with his mother. He would not tolerate her bad-mouthing Phoebe and she had to show her respect as his wife and the mother of his child. He also wanted an end to her phone calls about her health dramas, which usually ended in there being nothing wrong with her. He informed her that the next Christmas would be spent with Phoebe's parents.

It took Heather a few weeks to handle what had happened and initially she remained withdrawn. But she loved her son and her grandson, and recognised that she could end up alone and isolated from her family if she refused to compromise. She finally apologised to Phoebe.

————

TALKING ABOUT THE IN-LAWS

Before you take the quiz, it is important to reflect on three key areas. With the relationship with your in-laws (this includes brother and sister-in-law relationships) what are your expectations and hopes, and what is the reality? Invite your partner to do the same. This will really help you to talk about your relationships with both of your extended families and openly and honestly discuss any issues that might be harming you as a couple.

THE IN-LAWS QUIZ

1. Choose three words that best describe what kind of relationship you currently have with each in-law. (Are there any additional words?)
➤ Respectful, open, honest.
➤ Polite, civil, distant.
➤ Loving, close, supportive.
➤ Non-existent, painful, toxic.

2. From the same list, choose three words that best describe what kind of relationship you would like to have with your in-laws? (Are there any additional words?)

3. What expectations do you have of your in-laws?
➤ Babysitters.
➤ Money lenders.
➤ Emotional supporters.

➤ Friendship.
➤ Going on holiday together.
➤ Being together during the holidays.
➤ Inconvenient.
➤ A necessary chore.

4. So far, what is going well in your relationship with them?

5. So far, what is not going well in your relationship with them?

6. Would you say that your in-laws don't approve of you?

7. If yes, what don't they approve of? How does their disapproval show itself?

8. How supportive are you with your partner when it comes to your own parents' treatment of them?

9. How boundaried is your relationship with your own family?

10. If you could tell your in-laws to change one thing that would improve your relationship with them, what would it be?

11. If your in-laws could tell you to change one thing that would improve their relationship with you, what would it be?

Now, review your responses. Notice whether your hopes and expectations of the relationship with your in-laws actually match the reality. Notice whether the gap between hopes and reality is: pretty close, not bad but could be improved upon or miles apart.

Looking at the relationship this way will help to focus you on where changes can be made to improve the relationship and where compromises can be made.

Self-Help Tips: Managing Your Relationship with Your In-Laws

1. **Take the pressure off.** The key to a healthy relationship with your in-laws is to have a boundaried relationship that consists of mutual respect. Yes, I know that this is easier said than done! So if you approach it as a work in progress and remove the pressures of 'they should behave this way or that' or 'they ought to fit in' or 'they must always …', then you have a greater chance of cultivating a more meaningful bond.

2. **United front.** You and your partner need to be each other's greatest supporters and have a united front in order to create a healthy connection with the in-laws. There is no use your partner agreeing to support you or you agreeing to support them on a specific issue and then becoming silent and distancing yourself when it comes to speaking up in front of the in-laws.

3. **Listen to what your in-laws are saying.** Notice whether they are just being critical for the sake of putting you down. Is there pain behind the words that could indicate that they're feeling unhappy about something, yet feel unable to be honest with you? For instance, do they feel put upon to babysit every week without fail, but fear that if they say no you'll react badly and cut them off? Are you assuming that they should always be available to you? This may be a bitter reality to swallow, but it could save further resentment down the line if you sit down with them and check that they are okay with the way arrangements are.

ARE YOUR IN-LAWS TOXIC?

➤ Do you feel put down or 'less than' when you are with your in-laws?

➤ Are they judgemental and critical of you?

➤ Do they divide and rule by trying to separate you from their child?

➤ Are they two-faced? Nice to you, but behind your back abusive?

If you've noticed one or all of these things ringing true, then it is time to speak to your partner about it. In any relationship being undermined or mistreated is wrong and sadly it won't magically stop until someone steps in and stops it from continuing to happen.

It is crucial that your partner (who may well be *so* used to this behaviour that they've become immune to it) speaks up on your behalf and lays down a firm boundary. Being critical and judgemental may be their way of communicating with each other, but that doesn't mean it's acceptable!

Self-Help Tips: Avoiding Emotionally Explosive Encounters

If the benefits of the relationship far outweigh the costs, then compromises can be made.

1. Keep the time you spend in each other's company time-limited and stick to it.

2. Remain on safe topics of conversation.

3. Stay away from hot-button issues that you and your partner know will cause arguments with the in-laws.

4. Don't drink excessive amounts of alcohol as a coping strategy when you're in their company. Alcohol does loosen the tongue and there is an increased risk of saying things that you will later regret.

5. Don't leave communicating plans for family gatherings to the last minute. For instance, be clear three months in advance where you are planning to spend the holidays and who with. This will give everyone time to digest it, express their feelings, deal with it and then move on.

FERTILITY PROBLEMS

It is deeply painful to experience infertility and it can have an enduring emotional and psychological effect if you want children. Some couples aren't ever able to conceive, some may decide that adoption or fostering is not for them, and so remain childless. Studies on infertility describe how involuntary childlessness affects one in ten couples and is an 'on-going emotional pain'.[9]

Being childless can precipitate a deep sense of grief and loss. You and your partner may well experience and express your personal grief in very different ways – and the relationship may at times become very strained. Feelings of failure are common and you may handle the pain differently. One person may want to look for solutions to fix the problem and the other may feel unable to express their true feelings or may start to blame themselves. These feelings of loss and disappointment can be overwhelming and may lead to both of you hiding your deepest pain from one another. However, this strategy never works because feelings that are denied expression always become bigger and more troublesome.

Those around you can also be affected. This might be your parents realising that they'll never be grandparents. Friendships can suffer if you withdraw from people you care about because they have the family that you really want. Well-meaning friends may ask you to be godparents believing that they're being supportive, but which may leave you feeling angry and upset instead.

It is so important to be loving and open with each other and to recognise that there is no right or wrong way to feel and that this isn't about blame. Support for each other at such a difficult time is crucial.

———

Case Study: We Want a Family

Jimmy (35), a computer programmer, and Parminder (33), a receptionist, had been together for ten years. Jimmy's brother, Richie, was married to Parminder's eldest sister, Satpinder, and so they'd known each other for a long time.

They had a very happy and loving relationship and were planning on having lots of children. They took holidays together and enjoyed themselves. They started trying for a child when Parminder was 28. Her three sisters had nine children between them and she expected that she'd have no problem getting pregnant. After a frustrating year of trying and still not getting pregnant, she decided to pay her doctor a visit. He initially advised her to keep trying.

However, Parminder was becoming increasingly anxious to get pregnant and was frustrated by how long it was taking. She went to a private clinic for a second opinion. After a number of tests she was diagnosed with 'unexplained infertility'. This came as a terrible shock to her and Jimmy.

Shattered by the discovery, Parminder was initially numb. But gradually this gave way to depression. She was distressed that her siblings all had big families. Her closest sister, Satpinder, had only recently shared with her how she and her husband were currently arguing because he wanted another child and she didn't want any more – three children was enough for her. Parminder didn't want to tell her family what she and Jimmy were going through, and asked him to promise that they'd keep this news to themselves. They became consumed by wanting a baby and this became their only topic of concern and of conversation.

Parminder started to avoid family get-togethers and her once close relationship with her sisters became very distant. They tried talking to her because they could see the change in both her and Jimmy, but Parminder said she was fine.

Jimmy was grief-stricken. He hadn't considered that they'd have any difficulty having children and he began to feel strangely empty. He could see that Parminder was struggling to handle her feelings and just wanted her to feel better. Desperate to find a solution to handle his sense of helplessness, he tentatively suggested IVF. They'd been putting money aside every month towards starting a family and he felt that this money would be put to good use. After much discussion, they decided to embark on this route and went back to the private clinic.

Crunch Time

When the first cycle didn't work, Parminder felt able to rationalise it and try again, but after the third unsuccessful attempt she was totally devastated. She felt deeply as though she'd completely failed. Her body had failed her, and she'd failed Jimmy. She became increasingly withdrawn and lost a lot of weight.

Jimmy was so worried about her that he rang his brother and blurted it out to him. He knew he was letting Parminder down, but could no longer bear to see her in such awful pain. Although he felt guilty too, he also felt a huge sense of relief to finally share it with someone else.

Within days, the entire family knew about it. Parminder's sisters made an intervention and turned up at her home unannounced. She broke down, confessing that it was so difficult to see them because she felt so jealous of them. She shared how hard it was to go out as everywhere she looked she saw either pregnant women or babies in their buggies. She couldn't even bear to watch TV in case a baby advert came on.

Parminder felt so angry and betrayed by Jimmy because he'd revealed their secret to the rest of the family and for a while their relationship was very strained. Out of desperation, Jimmy suggested that they try some counselling as a couple to come to terms with what they were going through.

Through the sessions with the counsellor, Parminder and Jimmy started to acknowledge their grief. Parminder admitted that the reason she didn't want anyone else knowing that they were struggling to have a child was that by saying it out loud it became a painful reality. Jimmy shared that he felt isolated in his grief and helpless to know how to make things better. He also admitted that he couldn't bear to see the pain Parminder went through during IVF and was willing to forego parenthood because he loved her so much.

Jimmy

Jimmy recognised that in the relationship he was often the fixer and needed to take practical control in order to make things better. He had suggested IVF as a solution and hadn't really considered the emotional impact this could have on Parminder. He realised that she went along with this option to make him happy and to provide the family they'd always wanted. Parminder not being able to get pregnant had left him feeling helpless and useless. But, instead of talking to her about how he'd felt, he shared his feelings with someone else. He now understood how this could leave her feeling so let down by him.

Parminder

Parminder recognised that she tended to take emotional control. Her need to show her family that all was well had left her and Jimmy without the support that they could have benefited from. She wouldn't allow herself to admit things were wrong in her life and this was a familiar pattern of behaviour for her. She hadn't wanted to disappoint Jimmy nor could she cope with the sense of failure about being unable to get pregnant. So instead of sharing her doubts about wanting IVF she went along with it, stating very clearly that this was something that she was committed to doing in order to have a baby.

The Way Forward

Although they wanted the best for each other, both of them could see that their coping mechanisms were at odds with each other and, in this situation, were causing them pain.

After several sessions, the counsellor invited them to start refocusing their lives on more positive aspects. They'd spent so long wanting a child, focusing on it and grieving for what could have been that they'd forgotten to nurture and nourish their relationship.

Jimmy and Parminder felt a huge sense of relief when they heard this. It was as though someone had given them permission to take time off and think about something else. They decided to stop having IVF and made the decision to just book a holiday and take time out together. They spent three weeks away, talking, hugging, eating properly and being able to have sex with no agenda other than to be intimate and close to each other.

After three long years of distress and disappointment, Parminder and Jimmy made the tough decision to stop trying for a baby and refocus their energies. Trying so hard to have a child had become all consuming, and often deeply painful for them both. They recognised that their relationship had suffered a lot and they both acknowledged that this had caused them to lose sight of each other. They knew that they had a strong and loving bond. They agreed that it was time to reinvest in one another once again, and start to rebuild their relationship.

———

HANDLING YOUR FEELINGS

It is so important to get support so that, together with your partner, you can both come to terms with your feelings. Having counselling can help you both express how you feel in a safe space and provide you both with the opportunity to get the emotional support that you need.

THE STAGES OF GRIEF

Grieving for the loss of your longed-for child is completely normal. There are stages of grief, which are listed here as a guide to help you to recognise what you may be going through. They are by no means prescriptive. There is no timescale for how long it should take and feelings aren't linear, they can go back and forth.

➤ When you first get the news, the initial reaction is shock, numbness and denial. This can last hours, days or weeks.

➤ Once the numbness subsides, you may be hit by a deep sense of anger and longing. The anger may be about the loss of your hopes, dreams and future plans. You may get angry with yourself, your partner, friends and family.

➤ These feelings may then give way to deep sadness, depression and withdrawal from loved ones.

➤ Reframing and rethinking feelings signals the beginning of positive emotions. The sadness may subside and you may start to see light at the end of the tunnel. There may be pangs of grief, but there may also be happy moments starting to come through.

➤ Acceptance and moving on. This is the time when you may start engaging with interests and refocusing your life.

There will be times when you feel okay about it and are able to get on and enjoy your life, but there are other times when the loss of your longed-for child may feel acute. This is entirely normal. You may have adjusted to your friends becoming parents, only to re-experience the loss when friends start to become grandparents.

Being aware of the grief cycle can help you and your partner to understand and be mindful of your emotional triggers so that you can take care of yourself and of each other.

ANXIETY

We are all prone to bouts of anxiety and worry from time to time. Anxiety is a natural reaction to a situation that makes us feel fearful. Anxious feelings are a way of alerting us to the fact that something doesn't feel right for us. Some fears can be traced back to a specific negative event and some anxious feelings can result from a fear of what might happen. Sometimes a major life change or upheaval can prompt feelings of anxiety: such as divorce or separation, job loss, long-term illness or bereavement. Sometimes there is no obvious cause of the anxiety.

Anxiety can affect the emotional well-being of your relationship. For instance, anxieties about getting older, running out of time and regrets about lost opportunities may trigger a midlife crisis. This may alter the way you see yourself, how you behave towards your partner and your overall outlook. Or you may be worried about your job security and therefore have fears about your finances, worries about paying the mortgage and concerns about how you may support the family. This may result in tensions within the relationship.

Some people can experience prolonged anxiety, which can have very negative effects on health and well-being by interfering with day-to-day functioning – affecting sleep and eating habits as well as compromising the ability to concentrate properly. All these factors may eventually become debilitating and could lead to depression.

If you are prone to anxiety, then in the first instance it might be a great idea to keep a diary so that you can keep track of your triggers. Writing it down can help you to step back and observe whether the triggers are based on realistic things to get worried about or not.

AN ANXIETY SUFFERER'S DIARY

As an example, here is a page from Simon's diary:

➤ 9am: Noticed I was breathing faster as I approached the office. Had a performance meeting with my manager and felt anxious.

➤ 9.30am: Worried that the boss was going to be critical, heart racing, sweaty palms, so spent the meeting avoiding eye contact.

➤ 10.30am: Felt he'd been quite negative about my work, felt too angry to say anything.

➤ 11.00am: Had a row with a colleague who'd forgotten to email me an important document.

➤ 1.00pm: Missed lunch, headache coming on, had to finish a report.

➤ 3.30pm: Rushing to finish my report, I accidently deleted it.

➤ 5.45pm: Jumped in taxi to catch early train, which I then missed, because taxi was caught in a traffic jam. Felt furious.

➤ 8.00pm: Felt awful. Thumping headache, shouted at the kids, told them to go to bed.

➤ Didn't talk to my partner much, she could see I was angry.

➤ 9.45pm. Ate dinner quickly, didn't really taste it. Watched telly in silence.

➤ 11.00pm: Went to bed, mind racing, couldn't get to sleep properly.

Simon reviewed this diary with a counsellor. He was invited to step back and take on the role of an objective observer when recounting the performance review. He realised that his boss had actually praised him several times. He had suggested a couple of areas where Simon could improve, but these were minor points. Simon had dismissed the positive feedback and magnified the negative. He noticed that in his negative state he'd lost concentration and made mistakes, then taken his frustrations out on others by blaming and being critical of colleagues and family.

Case Study: I Need to Be In Charge

Eddie (46) and Molly (43) had been married for 18 years. Eddie worked as a senior police officer and Molly was a self-employed marketing consultant. They had two daughters, aged 12 and 14. They described their relationship as comfortable and pretty happy most of the time.

Eddie had been working longer and longer hours of late. Although he loved his job most of the time, he had been feeling under increasing pressure. There were rumours circulating about possible redundancies and although he had been told directly by his boss that he would not be in the firing line, Eddie felt anxious.

He became increasingly suspicious as to why his boss had arranged to have a meeting with him the following month. Eddie panicked and, in that time, managed to convince himself that he was going to be made redundant. However, he found it hard to share his fears with Molly or with any of his close friends and colleagues and ruminated on his concerns by himself. The more he worried about it, the more he convinced himself that he was absolutely right to be suspicious.

Molly noticed that he had become withdrawn and distant. But when she asked him about this, he assured her that everything was okay.

He often chose to go to bed later than her, complaining of exhaustion, or if he went to bed first, was fast asleep by the time she joined him. Molly was becoming worried; this was unusual behaviour for him, as they'd always had a close, intimate and healthy sex life. Although it was usually Molly who instigated sex, now, when she touched him, signalling that she wanted to make love, he just pulled away.

This behaviour continued to get worse and there was a lot of tension between them. Anything and everything was causing petty arguments. Eddie was getting tetchy with his daughters, picking up on every little thing they did, whether it was their untidy bedrooms, what they were wearing or having music on too loud.

Matters were made worse, when his boss postponed the meeting, putting it off for another fortnight. This was followed by the biggest breakdown in communication between Molly and Eddie when she was offered an exciting opportunity with a major company to manage three large perfume brands. Molly was absolutely delighted with this offer, as she had been headhunted by an old business associate of hers. When she shared the news with Eddie she had expected him to be happy for her, but instead he started asking lots of negative questions, such as: who would run the household? How could they both work long hours? Who would be there for the girls? He said that this wasn't great timing.

Eddie's reaction completely threw Molly. Her perspective was that they could now work towards paying off chunks of their mortgage, could put more money aside for the girls' college fund and perhaps even start saving more money again. Instead, Molly's good news saw Eddie become even more negative and distant.

Eddie

Eddie had always been the main earner in the family. Although Molly worked throughout their marriage, her consultancy work tended to be a less consistent source of income. Eddie saw himself as the more stable provider whose role was to support his family. As a result, they agreed as a couple that Eddie would have more control over the family finances than Molly. Although Molly had her own bank account, she agreed that with Eddie's regular income it was better that mortgage payments and regular bills went out of his account and she paid the food bills and for school trips and clubs, and contributed to the family holidays.

Eddie had always wanted to have an ordered and structured family life. It was what he was brought up in and he worked hard to recreate that familiar environment for himself and his own family.

Eddie's father had been in the army and was posted to numerous locations all over the world, which meant that the family had to regularly uproot themselves to make the move with him so that they could stay together. This was fine for Eddie and his older brother for a while, but as they got older it stopped feeling like an adventure and started to feel like a chore, because each time they settled down and made friends they'd have to move on again. As a result, Eddie's parents decided to send their sons to boarding school when they were aged 14 and 12 because they felt that their sons needed less disruption and a more stable base.

Eddie found it really hard at first and missed his parents dreadfully. However, he felt that he had to be grown up about it and deal with his parents' decision. His mother arranged to visit the boys as much as she could and they always spent school holidays together. She often asked them how they were doing and Eddie always expressed how happy and fun school was. However, whenever it came time to say goodbye to her he would almost always become very withdrawn and refuse to hug her.

Eddie found it incredibly difficult to talk about how he felt and wanted to be more like his older brother John, whom he experienced as tough and strong. John went on to train with the RAF as a pilot and law enforcement appealed to Eddie. He joined the police as soon as he was able to.

Molly

Molly grew up with two older brothers. Her parents owned and ran three clothes stores in the area. Molly described her parents as very entrepreneurial – willing to take risks, try new things out and they were very ambitious. Molly helped out at the shops as soon as she was old enough – doing stocktaking or helping out customers. Her parents' fortunes experienced great highs and devastating lows. There were times when things went well and the family enjoyed a good living, and times when things were tough. Molly clearly remembers the anxiety she experienced when two of the shops closed and the family had no choice but to cut back and downsize their lifestyle. The stress of money worries caused constant rows between her parents and eventually led to the breakdown of their marriage.

Molly longed for stability in her working life, but at the same time was attracted to doing things her own way. She wanted the autonomy of being her own boss and picking and choosing how she wanted to work. She had her parents' entrepreneurial spirit, but knew she needed more security.

When she and Eddie got together he was already well established in his career and she was attracted to his more stable, secure and structured approach. She also liked that he never stood in her way when it came to her being creative and ambitious in her work.

Crunch Time

Molly made up her mind to take the job whether she had Eddie's blessing or not. She felt angry that he'd become so distant and cold. Eddie knew on one level that he was being unreasonable, but just didn't know what to say to Molly. He loved her, but often found it excruciating to admit difficult feelings to her. He was worried about his job, had fears about losing his lifeline of work and this was causing him to have sleepless nights. He was avoiding Molly because the last few times they'd had sex he'd lost his erection, and although Molly tried to reassure him he felt as though he was not a proper man. He felt further emasculation when Molly got the job, because he imagined that she'd now have to support the family and he would no longer have a valuable role to play anywhere in his life.

One Saturday night, Eddie went to the pub with some of his friends and got blind drunk. He ended up spending the night at his mate's house, but in his state forgot to tell Molly where he was. She tried his mobile almost continuously through the night but it was switched off. She ended up contacting a colleague and family friend of theirs, worried that something dreadful had happened to him. When Eddie turned up the next morning dishevelled and hungover, Molly knew it was time to confront him.

This is how Molly found out about Eddie's job fears. She was shocked that he'd not shared any of this with her – even when she'd asked him directly many times – and she felt hurt and let down. Eddie admitted that he'd received a letter on the Friday requesting that he attend a consultation with an occupational health counsellor. He found out that a number of his colleagues had raised concerns about his behaviour.

The Way Forward

Eddie attended the counselling sessions. During the first meeting, Eddie was very defensive. He didn't feel safe talking about feelings or his personal life in this context and was deeply mistrustful. He knew there were issues that he wasn't handling, but he certainly wasn't about to air them here.

Eddie was assured that the sessions were confidential, so he slowly began to open up. He had four sessions on his own where he spoke about his anxieties about his job and his worries about being unable to support his family in the way that he wanted to, as well as an underlying fear that he and Molly may be drifting apart.

Eddie realised that him experiencing erectile dysfunction had started around the same time that he'd been feeling increasingly anxious about his job. It was compounded by Molly's career really taking off and his feelings of being redundant as a man escalated. His identity was very wrapped up in his occupation and fearing he could lose it left him feeling useless. He also had a real anxiety about disrupting his children's lives and causing them unhappiness, just as he'd experienced unhappiness himself as a young boy.

The counsellor asked Eddie if he'd like Molly to attend to talk things out. Eddie wasn't used to sharing his feelings with Molly, but he realised that he needed to let her in. He recognised that he had a long-held belief that telling people how you really felt only caused them pain, so what was the point of putting them through that? The counsellor demonstrated that by not saying how he felt, he and his family were already in pain.

As Molly and Eddie started to share more and work together as a team, the tensions at home decreased. They could see that they had both been feeling anxious, Molly about embarking on a new career and Eddie worried about the possibility of losing his job.

Molly postponed her start date by a few months in order to put practicalities in place that she and the rest of the family could work within.

Eddie saw his GP and discussed erectile dysfunction (ED) with him. After full tests, it was established that his ED was psychological and Eddie could do a number of things that could help towards managing it successfully. He was advised to pay attention to his diet, cut back on his drinking and continue to practise the anxiety-reducing techniques he'd learnt in the counselling sessions. Molly and Eddie decided to have some sessions of sex therapy so that they could continue to explore effective ways to communicate on a more intimate level.

Eddie finally got the news that his contract would remain the same for the next 18 months, but that there was a possibility of changes after that. Eddie felt better equipped to handle changes, because he now had a clearer understanding of what made him anxious as well as effective coping skills to manage his feelings so that he could more effectively deal with challenges that could come up.

———

Self-Help Tips: Dealing with Anxiety

The first step is to stop anxiety overwhelming you by shaking up your thinking.

1. First off, identify what you are really anxious about. Is it a real anxiety that you can do something about, or is it a background 'what if' worry?
2. Limit your worry time. Have 30 minutes to focus all your worry energy into. Write out the problems and then identify solutions. This will help you to gain a sense of control, as well as help to stop worries from taking over.
3. Be realistic. Set yourself manageable, achievable goals.
4. Get perspective. Sometimes the more you worry alone, the more the anxiety grows. Sharing how you feel with your partner can really help you to gain perspective.

5. Distract yourself. Simply focusing on one thing gives it power and energy to take over your day and overwhelm you. Engage in distracting activities – go for a walk or a swim, whatever you love to do.
6. Jot it down. If you have something you'd like to say, but feel anxious about saying it, then jot it down and rehearse saying it a few times. This will help you feel back in control and convey more confidence.

We all have 'what if' background worries from time to time. But if these are becoming intrusive and interfering with everyday life – like work, relationships or sleep – then seeing a counsellor to get to the root of what may be going on is crucial.

They can help you explore what could be at the root of your anxiety, as well as teach you techniques to help you manage it.

MAINTAINING A HEALTHY SEX LIFE

Sex is a natural part of a loving relationship. It helps you to reinforce your intimate physical and emotional bond with your partner. But as time goes on, maintaining a healthy sex life can at times feel like a challenge and sexual satisfaction can be affected by a number of things. Feeling stressed out, loss of libido, body image worries, the demands of your life-style, no time, no privacy, illness and relationship tensions can all affect your sex life with your partner. Also, boredom in the bedroom affects nearly all couples at some point in the relationship. The allure of your partner may have subsided, you may have got into a comfy-pair-of-slippers routine and sex may not seem worth bothering with.

I've also worked with a number of clients who associated sex with a means to have children, so it became something to be endured rather than to take pleasure in. Long-held beliefs like this have the potential to become problematic as the relationship goes on. Why? Because one person's difficulty in seeing sex as a pleasurable, intimate connection could be interpreted by their partner as loss of interest in them – potentially leading to emotional distancing between a couple.

Self-Help Tips: A Healthy Sex Life

1. Whatever the reason, it is so important to talk to your partner about how you feel. It sounds simple enough, but I know that it can feel like one of the toughest conversations to start, because feelings like shame or embarrassment may get in the way. But by not talking to each other you run the very real risk of an increasingly tense atmosphere.

2. Ensure you create the right environment – it is vital to make time to talk when you're both relaxed and able to focus on each other without distractions.

3. Don't blame or criticise, but start from a loving place. Often, what is at the root of sexual problems is relationship tensions, so talking to each other about what may be getting in the way is crucial.

4. By openly expressing feelings, you and your partner can also find out what other issues may be affecting you both: whether it is emotional, physical or relationship worries. That way, you can focus on what needs to be sorted out.

5. If boredom has taken over, or you've simply slipped into a predictable routine, then focus on what turns you on. Writing down and then sharing fantasies can charge up your sex life and inject excitement back into your love life.

6. If you've been too busy lately, make a point of increasing how much you hug, touch and kiss each other.

7. Don't make excuses; instead, make a date to make love. Putting the effort in is important and knowing that there is a date in the diary builds anticipation and excitement.

8. If you're feeling under pressure to perform, then it's important to step back and give yourself a break. The more you worry about how well you're doing, the more likely your anxiety will increase. Take your time to enjoy

being together, whether it is giving each other a sensuous massage, caressing, cuddling or even taking a shower together. This can bring back much-needed closeness and physical connection that can stimulate both of you and help you to reconnect again.

If there are health or physical issues that you need extra support with then talking to your GP can help.

GETTING EXTRA ADVICE

Sometimes a little extra help can be just the boost you need. Yes, I know, it might feel a bit embarrassing to take the initial step and open up to a therapist about your sex life, but think about it this way – their goal is to help you and your partner get to where you both want to be in your sex life. The potential positive benefits to you and your partner far outweigh a bit of initial blushing. Talking to someone like a sex therapist can be so useful on many levels: whether it is tackling issues from the past that may be preventing you from having a fulfilling sex life in the present, improving sexual communication with your partner, dealing with the impact of children, handling your changing body image, reframing beliefs about your own sexuality, breaking bad habits, spicing things up or learning to make time for each other. Your sex life is as good as you want it to be, so as a partnership investing time, effort and commitment will mean you both reap the benefits.

ERECTILE DYSFUNCTION
Some studies show that about 30–40 per cent of men aged between 40 and 70 experience moderate to severe erectile dysfunction and an additional 15 per cent may have a milder form.[10] There are physical as well as psychological causes of erectile dysfunction and these

symptoms can have a negative effect on a person's self-esteem, confidence and relationship. It is imperative to see a doctor, who can carry out a series of tests to determine the cause and suggest a way forward.

I know it can be embarrassing for a man to approach a doctor about this issue. But if it's hurting your relationship and causing you to feel bad about yourself, then it's time to take a deep breath, jot your symptoms down and share them with your doctor.

There are possible psychological causes of erectile dysfunction, for instance: performance anxiety, being worried or feeling depressed, or if you've lost your job. Physical symptoms can be brought on by certain medications or illnesses.

If your GP identifies the cause as psychological then take steps to track your triggers and reduce your anxiety and stress levels (see pages 237–8 on how to do this).

When communication with your partner breaks down and you feel as though your relationship has become more adversarial, then being together can feel like the most challenging place to be. Problems can manifest themselves in different ways, whether it is physical or emotional symptoms. The key is to become aware of what the triggers may be and communicate openly and honestly with your partner in order to reconnect and work together again, so that you can become each other's greatest source of support. It is so important for your emotional well-being and helps to make difficulties less daunting and challenges more manageable.

Chapter 9
Growing Older Together

Different life stages bring about the opportunity to revisit who we are as individuals, where we are in our lives and who we are now in our relationship. When it comes to aging, I think that if you asked, most people would talk about getting older with some degree of mixed feelings. Some people may imagine it as something to worry about, perhaps through experiencing it second-hand through their aging parents, or they may have internalised the negative myths that society projects on to older people. Other people may have a more positive outlook and therefore feel able to embrace getting older and look forward to working less, having their children off their hands, having the chance to experience new adventures and start a new chapter in their relationship.

Getting older is something we all have in common and yet it is a deeply personal experience and process. Who you are as a person, what you have learnt about yourself so far, how you deal with challenges, your attitude to life, choices you've made so far, as well as your own beliefs about what it means to get older, will all inform how you handle the future. Physical, psychological and emotional challenges cannot be avoided, whether it is coping with your changing body (including for women going through menopause), facing the reality of your children growing up and leaving home, or if you've chosen not to have a family facing the reality that when you and your partner are no longer here that will be the end of the line. Other challenges include caring for aging parents, retirement, a partner's illness or the loss of a parent or partner.

You and your partner may be looking forward to your future together once the children have become more independent, only to find that they're struggling to get started and you have to step in and help them out financially or practically. Some couples also have to face pressures from both sides – as parents live longer and children struggle to get on to the property ladder or get employment. Those who experience this now common upward and downward pressure have been called the 'sandwich generation'.[11]

It's no wonder, then, that some of us may choose not to think about getting older and just let it happen.

As a strategy, avoiding thinking about getting older or preparing for the future can work in the short term, but later on it can feel like psychologically 'hitting the wall' when changes inevitably happen. You may have got to this life stage without having had major issues to deal with, only to find that changes in health, the loss of a partner or children becoming more independent bring about big emotional challenges. You may have been so busy focusing on raising a family and building your career that inherent relationship difficulties may have got pushed to one side and avoided until life changes force you to confront issues later on.

In this chapter, I am going to focus on how to handle the changes during this life stage. This chapter will help you to take steps both to manage getting older or plan and prepare for your future in a constructive, positive and realistic way. I will also focus on aspects like creating and maintaining positive friendships, continuing to be productive in your life, looking after your health and mental well-being – factors that can all contribute to having a happier experience and an energised and positive relationship with your partner.

TAKING STOCK OF YOUR LIVES TOGETHER

Before you can plan and prepare for the future, you need to have a clear picture of who you are now, how you are experiencing your relationship so far and what your personal thoughts, feelings, beliefs and attitudes are about getting older. These questions are relevant to you whether you are single at this point in your life or have a partner.

QUICK QUIZ: TAKING STOCK

1. About you.

➤ How often do you think about getting older?
   All the time. Some of the time. Seldom. Never.

➤ When you do think about getting older, what words come to mind?
   For example: doddery, slow, wise, exciting, tired, experienced, grumpy, happy, free, relief, sick, fed-up, restricted. Any other words?

➤ When you think about getting older what feelings come to mind?
   For example: fear, happy, fun, scary, worried, joyful, carefree. Any other words?

➤ When you see your changing body, how do you feel? How do you feel about the lines on your face?

➤ What relationship do you have with yourself now? When you look back at photos of yourself, how do you feel about that person in the photo compared to who you are now?

➤ What (if anything) do you miss about your younger self?

➤ What (if anything) do you celebrate about yourself now?

---

2. Your life now.
➤ How satisfied do you feel with your life so far?
Very satisfied. Satisfied. Dissatisfied. Very
dissatisfied.
➤ How often do you think about the past and what
could have been?
All the time. Sometimes. Seldom. Never.
➤ How often do you think about goals that you never
reached?
All the time. Sometimes. Seldom. Never.

3. Your relationship now.
➤ On a scale of 1 to 10 (1 = unhappy 10 = very
happy), how happy/unhappy are you in your
relationship right now?
➤ Describe what three things you value about your
partner.
➤ Describe what aspects of your relationship you have
grown to accept over time.
➤ How much closer do you feel to your partner now?
➤ What positive changes have occurred in your
relationship so far?
➤ What challenging changes have occurred in your
relationship so far?
➤ What do you cherish about your relationship?
➤ When you and your partner look at old photos
together, what feelings come up for both of you?
Happy memories. Longing for the past. Regret.
➤ What three beliefs do you hold about yourself and
about your partner?
For instance:
Myself   *My partner*
I am the reliable one. My partner is the rock.
I am the provider.   My partner is the carer.

➤ How much do you have in common? Consider friends, hobbies, interests, travel.

➤ Have you over the years:
Grown together? Shifted apart? Put up with each other?

4. Your future self.

➤ Project yourself into the future. How do you imagine your life will be in five years from now, in ten years from now?

➤ How do you imagine your relationship *with yourself* will be?

➤ If your older self could advise you on one thing that you should prepare for right now, what would that be?

5. You and your partner.

➤ How do you imagine your relationship with your partner will be in five and ten years?

➤ How would you like your relationship with them to be? For instance: sharing adventures, travelling the world, moving to a smaller house, spending more time together, having a positive companionship, becoming more like friends, having a healthy, intimate and sexual relationship, can't imagine growing old together, resigned to staying together, being with someone you feel comfortable with, having separate lives but living under the same roof.

➤ How do you feel/does your partner feel about becoming a grandparent?

6. Your financial picture.

➤ How do you feel about retiring from work?

> ➤ How do you feel about your partner retiring from work?
> ➤ How do you feel about the possibility of having to change your life as you get older? For instance: downsizing, having less income, spending less money, relocating.

This quiz will give you a snapshot of your relationship journey so far, what you've learnt, what you've accepted, what your concerns are and what you'd still like to achieve.

Notice where your responses are negative and where they are positive. It is normal to have some concerns, but if over half of your responses are flagging up worries and concerns, then it is important to step back and make a note of what is worrying you and how you are handling those worries so far.

This is a fantastic opportunity to sit down with your partner and share your feelings and thoughts together. It's important to reflect on what attitudes you both have about getting older, how you see yourself and how see each other. You may have carefully planned and prepared for your financial future, but what about preparing for your emotional future?

These questions will help you realise where the negative feelings may be coming from. Notice whether you and your partner mostly believe that it's too late to change or whether you mostly have the willingness to embrace change and seize opportunities to continue to learn, to grow and to revitalise your life.

If you discover that you and your partner have, on the whole, a positive outlook, are willing to be flexible in your approach to life and look forward to your future together, then that's wonderful.

If the road ahead seems difficult and you've identified underlying problems and challenges that may be getting in the way of positive change, then there are self-help strategies that can help to provide you with a constructive way forward. First, though, I'm going to look at some of the more common issues that occur.

DRIFTING APART

There is no doubt that maintaining a long-term healthy relationship takes continuous work and effort from both parties. However, sometimes we get so caught up in the rhythm of daily life that we may have stopped prioritising our partner. We might ignore problems by distracting ourselves with the needs of others, bury ourselves in work or busy ourselves focusing on the children so much that we neglect to nourish our relationship, believing that somehow it will take care of itself.

But, if this happens we may then wake up one morning and wonder who the person lying next to us is. We may over time start to lose that special emotional connection and slowly begin to drift apart. At first this drift may not seem all that important, it is often when children leave home that we seriously notice it, as we're left facing a person we no longer recognise. Some couples experience this as a growing sense of emptiness in their relationship, or a feeling of loneliness even when their partner is in the same room.

Reconnecting with your partner when you begin to experience these type of feelings is so crucial to ensure that the drift doesn't become fatal to the relationship.

EMPTY NEST SYNDROME

One of the more vulnerable relationship times is when children leave home either to go to college or permanently move out. This can bring about a mixture of emotions, as it signifies the end of a particular life stage in the parent/child relationship, and the beginning of an emotional and practical shift in the family dynamics. This phase can sometimes bring about feelings of loss for parents commonly known as the empty nest syndrome.

Parents experience empty nest syndrome to different degrees. Some people describe it as suddenly feeling redundant, lost or rudderless. Other people feel sad, but are able to bounce back fairly quickly. Experiencing these feelings of loss can affect your relationship too.

Self-Help Tips: Practical and Emotional Preparation for Children Leaving the Nest

1. Preparation is the key to managing the emotional changes for both you and your child. If they're planning to go to college in a year, or move out to live independently, then start preparing now.
2. Focus on the positive steps that they are taking in their life.
3. Acknowledge that you will miss them. Be honest that although it will be a challenge for the whole family at first, it will also be a wonderful opportunity for growth and adventure. This will give your children psychological permission to feel able to grow and move on.

Focus on You

1. Your children will already be becoming more independent. Use this time to focus on reconnecting with old friends or start engaging in new interests and making new friends.
2. If you don't work, think about doing volunteering. Voluntary work can be very rewarding as well as give you the opportunity to mix with like-minded people.

Extra Support

However, when your kids do leave, prolonged grief could suggest that something else is going on. It is so important to:

1. Talk to your partner, because it is very likely that they are feeling the same way.
2. Get support from friends. Friends are very important to well-being and spending time together is good for you.
3. Be aware that if you are feeling low a lot of the time and you're not getting any better, then a positive step would be to talk to a professional counsellor, who may be able to help you express your feelings in a safe and non-judgemental space.

Case Study: Intimate Strangers

Gill (54) and Simon (59) had been married for 30 years. They had two daughters, Jane (18) and Kate (28). They described their relationship overall as comfortable. Simon had been the main breadwinner and Gill had devoted herself to bringing her daughters up. Simon had been in middle management in banking, but had recently lost his job and was struggling to get another one, and Gill now worked part-time in a charity shop. She had a wide circle of friends and spent a lot of her social time with close female friends.

When Gill and Simon got together in their twenties, Gill had just broken up with Neil, whom she described at the time as the love of her life. He had decided that he wasn't ready to settle down with her or anyone else and Gill had been left totally devastated. Neil moved out of the flat they shared together and had sent his friend Simon round to pick up the remainder of his things. When Gill met Simon she was at a very low point. She had only just started a career in nursing, wasn't enjoying it at all, was living in a place that she didn't really like and was in a state of shock about the abrupt ending of her relationship.

Simon was very attracted to Gill and within a few months they'd started seeing each other. Gill really liked the fact that Simon was solid and kind and that he wanted her. Simon loved everything about Gill – from her energy to her looks. He felt happy when he was with her and missed her when they were apart.

However, their relationship had faced a crisis early on when Gill came across Neil socially, a year after she'd married Simon. Neil confessed that he'd been wrong to end the relationship with her and, although he knew he couldn't have her back now, felt terrible about hurting her so badly. Gill was completely taken aback by this and found she still had powerful feelings for Neil. This culminated in them having an affair that lasted a few months. Gill realised afterwards that this was a huge mistake. She hated lying to Simon and felt as though she'd really messed things up and she decided to confess to him what she had done. This was a very difficult and painful make-or-break period. Simon became very withdrawn and they barely spoke. After a few months of soul-searching, Simon decided that the relationship was worth saving and they decided to start a family. Simon struggled with trust issues for quite some time after this and Gill went out of her way to persuade him that it was a horrible mistake, one that she deeply regretted.

Once their first child Kate was born, being parents became the central focus for Gill and Simon and their relationship settled into a comfortable pattern. There was a big gap in age between Kate and her sister Jane. Gill hadn't been sure whether she wanted to have another child and although Simon had mentioned wanting to have more children, it hadn't been something that they'd really spoken about. When Gill became pregnant at 35, she felt that perhaps this would bring her and Simon closer again. She'd felt that their relationship had been drifting apart for a while, but hadn't known what to say to Simon. Whenever she'd asked Simon if he was happy, he'd always said yes.

Jane became the focus of the family's attention and Kate doted on her younger sister.

When Kate moved out at 20, Gill felt that at least she still had Jane at home for a while longer and focused a lot of her attention and energy on her youngest.

Gill

Gill was the youngest of four children, the only girl. Her parents weren't particularly close and she remembers a lot of instability and chaos at home. Her mum was almost always threatening to end the marriage, and often expressed deep anger. Gill never really understood why her mother was so angry. Her mother's treatment of her was often very inconsistent and unpredictable. She could be loving one minute and lashing out and critical the next. Gill worked hard to gain her mother's approval, but without ever really knowing what would please her. Her father, although loving, was often silent and was more in the background of family life. He died aged 65 of a heart attack a few weeks after he retired from work.

When Gill's mother became ill, Gill decided to move her into the family home and took on the full responsibility of caring for her. Simon worried that this was the wrong thing to do. He couldn't understand why Gill wouldn't ask her brothers to share the responsibility, but agreed to support whatever she wanted to do. However, Gill's mother was demanding and critical, and Gill often felt drained and unappreciated. Their relationship remained fraught and unresolved right to the end. This created more tensions between Gill and Simon, and he often felt helpless and caught in the middle of mother and daughter.

Before Simon, Gill had often had short, intense love affairs with emotionally distant men. This led her to often feel mistrustful of them on the one hand, but on the other desperate for their approval and attention. A dynamic very similar to her relationship with her own parents.

Her relationship with her ex, Neil, had been inconsistent. It was sometimes loving and passionate, sometimes cold and distant, and she was never sure where she stood. Gill often felt insecure and uncertain about the relationship, but clung to it, admitting that she'd often felt worthless without Neil. Although her feelings caused her distress, they were familiar to her and she knew how to deal with it. What was unfamiliar and strange to her was being loved consistently by Simon. She found this very uncomfortable and was often looking for clues that he would suddenly become cold towards her. When he didn't behave in this way, she would feel ill at ease.

Although she'd grown to love Simon deeply, and becoming a mother had positively impacted on her emotional world, she was stuck in a negative life script. She felt unworthy of love because she saw herself as undeserving, yet she felt desperate to be loved and approved of. She sometimes felt as though she had one foot in the home and the other ready to flee.

Simon

Simon grew up in a very strict and traditional home. He had three younger brothers whom he was close to, and had a lot of friends at school and at the church choir he belonged to. His father was the local vicar and he remembers his father definitely being the head of the family and his mother very much in the supportive role. He remembers firm boundaries and a lot of rules, which centred on how to behave in public, always being polite and courteous to others, and how to properly represent the family wherever they went. Simon admired his father, who he described as always being kind and supportive to people in the local community and who instilled in him the message of being fair minded and forgiving. He was very close to his mother, but sometimes felt angry with her because he witnessed her putting the needs of others before her own so many times.

His relationship history reflected a very supportive and loving person, who sometimes stayed in relationships longer than he should have – usually out of pure loyalty to his girlfriends. He had a tendency to remain friends with them and if they ever needed help he would drop everything, which sometimes led to him being taken advantage of. It was not uncommon for him to lend money to ex-girlfriends who promised to repay him but never did. Although he felt angry and used, he'd learnt to be so emotionally controlled that this prevented him from expressing his true feelings.

With his own family, Simon was devoted to Gill and his daughters. When it came to disciplining his children, he always tried to be even-handed and usually left being strict to Gill. This meant that his daughters almost always came to him whenever they wanted something, because they knew he would easily give in.

When it came to Gill, Simon carried an underlying anxiety that he wasn't good enough for her and he sometimes asked her why she married him, because she could have had the pick of the crop. When she'd had the affair with Neil, he had felt totally devastated and, although over time he had forgiven her, he felt that on some level he was partly to blame. He'd never really shared with Gill how her betrayal had affected him and as time went on he'd found it harder and harder to admit his feelings, burying his distress instead. He promised Gill that he'd drawn a line under it and moved on.

Crunch Time
When Jane left for university, Gill and Simon both felt her loss deeply. It was only a few months after Gill's mother had died and she was experiencing very mixed emotions about her mother. At times she was relieved that her mother had gone, then she'd feel guilty for feeling this way and sometimes she'd feel deep sorrow.

She started feeling very sad whenever she was in the house alone, and started to avoid being there. She'd spend hours wandering around the shops or sitting in coffee shops just to distract herself. Although she shared how she felt with her closest friend, she didn't talk to Simon about it because she didn't want to burden him with any more worries. She knew that moving her mother in had added extra pressure on the whole family. Simon himself tried to stay focused on looking for another job, choosing to spend time at the local library to avoid the emptiness at home. He felt resentful towards Gill for overburdening him with the responsibility of her ailing mother, who in his eyes had been abusive and demanding, but because he felt that Gill needed his support he didn't say anything to her. However, he interpreted her unwillingness to talk to him as a sign that she didn't care how he felt – and this deepened his sense of loneliness.

Simon missed Jane a lot – they had similar interests, a similar sense of humour, and from when she was very young they'd had their special father–daughter ritual of going to watch their local football team together.

One Sunday afternoon, Simon just sat down in Jane's old room and quietly wept. Gill couldn't bear to see him like this and for the first time they talked honestly. Simon admitted that he feared that all he and Gill had in common these days were their daughters, and now with Jane moving on he just felt a big void. He was also fearful for the future, having been made redundant, and he told her how alone he felt. They talked about their own relationship and noticed how their lives had drifted apart. They didn't talk much any more and in the last six months Gill had been consumed with looking after her mother. She confessed that lately she preferred to spend time away from Simon and couldn't put her finger on why.

Gill had asked Simon to sleep in the spare room a couple of years earlier, as when she was going through the menopause she'd experienced symptoms like night sweats and periods of insomnia and she'd felt bad about ruining Simon's sleep. The trouble was that they remained in separate beds long after Gill's physical health had improved. They never discussed it, but slid into the habit of going their separate ways each night.

The Way Forward

Both of them could see that they needed support to work through the changes in their lives, because if they remained the way they were, they were in danger of growing apart completely and making each other miserable. They agreed to have counselling, even though Gill wasn't entirely convinced that it would help them.

However, it was a relief to both of them to hear that children leaving home could create feelings akin to a loss and that how they were both feeling was normal. One part of their parenting role was over, now that their youngest was becoming more independent of them.

Gill and Simon explored their own relationship resources and discussed what they did to nourish and nurture their relationship. It became clear to Gill and Simon that they had put all their loving energy into their children, but in the process had allowed their relationship to stagnate. When it came to intimacy, both of them admitted that they didn't have sex any more. They didn't really hug or touch each other much – perhaps the odd peck on the cheek. They admitted that they tended to talk about their daughters rather than share feelings with one another about their own relationship.

With counselling, Simon opened up about not ever really feeling that he matched up to Gill's expectations of her ideal husband – made worse now by his job loss. He saw himself now as half a man. Reflecting on Gill's affair, he admitted that although he'd forgiven her, he hadn't expressed his distress and anger to her. He admitted to experiencing multiple losses: his job, his children and the loss of his marriage.

Simon recognised that he was anxious about being honest with Gill for fear of losing her. However, he admitted that his unassertive approach and willingness to forgive her without ever expressing anger, while at the same time continuing to suffer in silence, enabled him to behave like the martyr in the marriage.

Gill explored her own beliefs about herself that she traced back to her relationship with her parents. She described seeing herself as insecure and drawn to anyone who showed her a grain of affection, which meant that she was often attracted to the wrong kind of people who messed her around and she clung to bad relationships because she felt that she didn't deserve any better.

Gill and Simon realised that they were no longer able to mask uncomfortable feelings by using a familiar pattern of behaving and diverting attention to other areas simply to avoid painful feelings and each other. They now had the opportunity to face and express their own vulnerabilities. Gill and Simon made a list of what they wanted to improve to make their relationship more positive and shared this list with each other. This formed the basis of their commitment plan.

The Commitment Plan

➤ They agreed that they needed to spend more time together.
➤ Simon wanted Gill to fully commit to being with him and they agreed that Simon would move back into the main bedroom.

➤ *Gill wanted Simon to speak his mind and be open and honest with her, so that she could support him.*

➤ *Gill wanted them both to go out and socialise together as a couple.*

➤ *They both agreed that their intimacy had all but fizzled out due to a lack of effort on both sides and they committed to making it a priority.*

Over a period of several months, and with effort and commitment on both sides, Gill and Simon began to see improvements in their relationship. They talked and shared how they felt far more than they'd ever done in their whole marriage. They went to bed at the same time so that they could talk, cuddle and begin to get close again.

––––––

RETIREMENT

Learning to spend time together again when one or both of you stops working is very important. Over the years of work, you would have developed routines and a way of living that worked beautifully. Suddenly finding each other in the house every day can have a negative impact.

A client of mine who was in her late fifties expressed how angry she felt whenever she saw her husband sitting in the armchair first thing in the morning. She explained how they'd both been looking forward to him retiring so that they could spend more time together. He'd officially retired a couple of months earlier and was enjoying the novelty of not having to rush to catch the early train to commute into work and looking forward to having breakfast with his wife instead. However, she couldn't stand seeing him in her space, messing up her highly organised routine. She felt obliged to make breakfast for him and sit with him while he read the morning papers. She felt as though her life had gone out of sync and she had trouble coming to terms with the changes. Digging a little deeper, we explored what was behind her anger. She had expressed a few worries to her close friends about having him in her space every day, but hadn't really confronted the concerns. His euphoria at stopping working and her anxiety about how to handle their relationship from now on had started to cause tensions in the home.

She recognised that having him at home had not only made her feel older but also prompted her to confront the changes in their life together. She'd freeze-framed him as the go-getting and energised working man and seeing him relaxed brought about feelings of anxiety for her. She'd got used to cultivating a life for herself, with its own rhythm. She worried about what they'd talk about now and wondered if she should start spending more time with him. They'd never talked to each other about how they'd both cope with the changes once he'd stopped working, they'd simply hoped for the best and this lack of communication had brought about an emotional crisis for her.

Self-Help Tips: Planning for Retirement Together
1. It is a very positive step to prepare for retirement at least five years before it actually happens – that way, you will have cultivated hobbies and interests so that by the time you stop working you have other things in place to put your energies into.
2. Plan now, for your future self. Make a list of things you'd like to do – whether it is learning a new language, taking up cooking lessons or doing more travelling.
3. Talk to your partner about what interests you can cultivate together so that you spend time together and have interests in common that you can share.
4. Choose and then emulate a positive mentor. This could be anyone you admire who has coped with changes and challenges in a constructive way.

My mentor is my wonderful father-in-law. He had been happily married for 35 years. In her latter years my mother-in-law became very ill with cancer and Alzheimer's. He devoted himself to nursing her at home right to the end. Within a couple of years of her death, and in his late sixties, he made the decision to relocate nearer to family and start again. He got involved with his passion for research, he joined the history society, researched his family tree, gave talks, made numerous friends, enjoyed the opera and managed to start a fulfilling new relationship. He took aging in his stride and proved that his positive and resilient attitude was the key to his enduring strength.

THE GRIEF OF ILLNESS

Becoming very ill can come as a terrible shock and be very traumatic. For some people it can feel like a huge loss. It is completely normal to go through a whole range of emotions.

How you experience the effects of illness is deeply personal and it is influenced by who you are as a person, and how you deal with challenges. However, there are some common emotional reactions that are entirely natural – and it is important to be aware of these.

THE CYCLE OF GRIEF WHEN BECOMING VERY ILL
➤ At first there may be a period of shock, as you come to terms with what has happened.
➤ You may experience a number of fears that the illness has brought with it: fear of leaving a loved one behind, fearing that you're losing control.
➤ There may be intense feelings of helplessness where you may feel defeated by what has happened to you.

> ➤ You may experience a sense of grief about losing your health, about a loss of status if you're no longer able to live or work the way you used to or by having to give up certain activities that you love.
> ➤ You may feel guilty that you're now a burden on your partner or your family and having caused pain and worry to those around you.
> ➤ It's not unusual to feel a sense of shame – as if some weakness has been exposed and you now have to rely on other people.
> ➤ You may feel anger with family members who may become overprotective and want to do everything for you.
> ➤ You may want to withdraw from everyone and want be left alone. There may be changes in your relationship as you pull away from your partner.

Case Study: Let's Talk

Daniel (64) and Ellen (60) had been together for 35 years. They had four children – three sons and one daughter. Daniel had had a long and successful career as a GP and three of his children had followed in his footsteps into the medical profession. His youngest son had chosen a career in graphic design. Ellen had spent many years as a freelance interior designer.

Daniel and Ellen had met while Daniel was travelling around America with friends before starting a new job back home at the local hospital. Ellen was from Boston and was visiting her family in New York when she and Daniel came across each other in a bar. They had a long-distance relationship for a few months, which proved difficult for both of them as Daniel worked long hours and couldn't really take time off to visit Ellen.

She made the decision to come to the UK and to see whether their relationship was worth investing in. They realised very quickly that they were deeply in love and she decided to stay.

Their marriage had a few challenges in the beginning. Daniel was very focused on his career and they had little time together. Ellen had to adjust to her big move and worked hard to make a life for herself. Once the children came along Ellen became a full-time mother and their lives settled into a pattern. They were very happy together, and Ellen's only complaint was that she wished Daniel was at home more. However, Daniel was very ambitious and over the years he and three colleagues set up a GP practice and focused on making that a big success. He wanted his children to have a legacy and his ambition for them was to take over his practice when he retired.

Crunch Time

Daniel had planned to retire when he was 65 and hand the reins of his practice to his eldest son. However, things didn't go according to plan. He was forced to take early retirement at 62 when one day at work he had a mild heart attack. He had been suffering from high blood pressure and was overweight. He had started drinking a little more than normal, telling Ellen that this was to help him sleep at night. Before his heart attack she had noticed that he was more short tempered of late and was very tightly wound.

Daniel had a very difficult time recuperating at home. The shock of the heart attack and being at home and being told to rest had affected him very badly. He felt scared, useless and agitated. He had been told to change his diet, lose weight and cut back on his drinking. Daniel was used to being in control and advising other people what to do; he couldn't stand feeling out of control and helpless.

A few months later, when the family had got together for Christmas, Daniel drank too much and became uncharacteristically confrontational. His family were deeply worried about him and at a loss as to what to do. They were afraid to say anything to him, for fear of upsetting him and bringing on another heart attack.

Ellen had accepted that at the moment he was very reluctant to have sex, because he too was fearful of another attack, but she was beginning to feel that their relationship was suffering. His behaviour had worsened and he was refusing to listen to her or his children's pleas that he needed help. She decided to take matters into her own hands and made an appointment for him to see his doctor.

He reluctantly agreed to go and talk things through and it was during this conversation that his GP suggested to him that he may benefit from some counselling support. Daniel was incredibly resistant at first as he saw this as additional failure.

The Way Forward

Over the course of several sessions, Daniel focused on what he'd been through. It became clear that he was experiencing an emotional crisis. He admitted that he felt lost, cut adrift and useless. He had poured so much of his energy into his work and he loved what he did and hadn't been ready to stop. He saw his heart attack as the beginning of the end. His life was over.

His core belief about himself was that he was capable, in charge and the backbone of the family. His heart attack had left him feeling physically and emotionally weak. He admitted that he hated being taken care of because that was his role in the family and he couldn't bear the loss of status. He hated the thought of his children having to see him as helpless and having to step in and support him.

Daniel recognised that his whole identity had become synonymous with being powerful, in charge, strong, and that getting ill suddenly threw this identity into turmoil. Daniel admitted that being sick at home left him feeling helpless – and he'd continued to drink in order to drown out these negative feelings. He felt as though he was rebelling against his own weakened body.

Daniel talked about his wife and his children and how wonderful they were; it was at this point that he broke down in tears. He saw that he'd been so busy providing for them that he hadn't stopped to truly be with them in the moment. He'd missed certain events in their lives that he'd regretted not making time for. He had become so *future focused that the present was slipping away. Daniel began to reflect on the possibility that his health shock was more of a wake-up call and an opportunity to approach his life differently from now on.*

Over time, Daniel started to make simple changes in his life. With the support of his family, he started taking better care of himself. He and Ellen joined the local leisure centre and decided to go swimming together once a week. They made changes to their diet and committed to going for a walk together three times a week. These small steps helped them both of them to start feeling physically healthier and emotionally connected to each other once more. Ellen felt that she'd got her husband back and that now they were able to move on with their lives in a more positive way.

———

Self-Help Tips: Handling the Grief of Illness

1. **Keep talking.** It is vital to keep communicating with your family. Any shock to one person in the family affects everyone in the family and the emotional ripple effect can bring out different reactions. Your partner and your children may also feel traumatised and experience a sense of loss themselves. They may feel anxious, sad or angry about what has happened to you. All these feelings are totally understandable and normal. It is important to acknowledge these feelings and, just like handling any other loss, it is crucial to seek out support from each other in order to recover. Loss of health can change how you relate to yourself and for some can bring about a loss of status, loss of self-respect and low self-worth. It is critical not to isolate yourself.

2. **Extra help.** If you need extra support, it is important to talk to your GP, who may refer you for some counselling sessions so that you can come to terms with what you are going through.

3. **Reframing.** It can be a bitter blow if circumstances have placed physical limits on you, but it is vital to focus on

where and how you can adapt and be more flexible. Concentrating on what you *can* do, rather than what you can't will help refocus your energies more positively.

4. **Make time for friends.** The benefits of having a good network of friends around you is well known. A recent study,[12] found that having more friends who we actually meet up with is important to our mental health and not having friends at all is bad for our mental health. It is important therefore to maintain your friendships and create opportunities where you can get out and meet new people.

If you need support to get out and engage in activities that you've always loved to do, but need a bit of extra help getting there and back, then ask family and friends. If you're feeling isolated and haven't got family support around you, then organisations like Age UK can be a wonderful resource for advice. See Further Help, pages 271–4.

SEX AND INTIMACY

You and your partner may have very different sexual needs. Women may lose interest in sex earlier than men – statistics published in the *British Medical Journal* showed that among 75–85 year olds 40 per cent of men and 17 per cent of women are sexually active. Many factors like illness, medication, feeling tired or loss of interest can affect your sex life, and if this is causing you problems then speak to your doctor for advice. According to medical advice, good general health boosts sex drive and enjoyment.

Our society projects the myth that sex is only for the young, which simply isn't true! You're never too old to enjoy a healthy sex life with your partner. If you've gone out of synch with one another or simply given up on it, then talk to your partner about what you can do to stay connected and close. Sex is just one way of sharing intimacy and affirming your loving bond. Holding hands, cuddling and kissing also help to strengthen your emotional bond.

Self-Help Tips: Nurturing Your Relationship at any Age

It is vital to continue to build and nurture your bond with each other. This is what helps make love last. Don't assume that just because you've made it this far you can simply stop trying.

1. Invest in simple tokens of affection – like holding hands, hugging, kissing and reminding your partner that you love them.
2. You may have spent years arguing back and forth, and expending a lot of energy on wanting to prove your points to each other. However, in order to have a successful relationship it is vital to choose your battles. Wasting energy on useless arguments can become corrosive and emotionally draining. Instead, focus on what really matters and ditch getting het up about your partner forgetting to buy the milk. Take a deep breath and then ask yourself: on a scale of 1 to 10 does this really matter, or would I just be winding the both of us into a frenzy for nothing?

    1 = it doesn't really matter at all,

    10 = it is too important to ignore.

    This will help you quickly work out what to do next.
3. Continue to be curious and interested by investing in hobbies that you love. It creates great balance if you can have hobbies and interests that you can both share, as well as interests that you can pursue as individuals.

OVER TO YOU

Every relationship is unique and has its own mixture of psychological and emotional influences, tensions, challenges and rewards. It takes love, commitment and sustained effort on both sides for a relationship to maintain its spark, its energy and its life force.

So, with your partner, write down three essential ingredients each that give you both shared joy and the spark that keeps you positively connected to each other.

Then, having written these down, put them in a place where you can both see them – as a wonderful gift: a visual reminder of what you treasure, appreciate and mean to each other.

Conclusion

Throughout the journey in this book, I have illustrated that at every stage of a relationship there are highs and lows. There may be times when you are faced with challenges that can test your resilience; tensions and differences that need to be worked through; crises that demand more of you; as well as times that are full of joy and are highly rewarding. All these aspects have the potential to enrich your relationship.

It is my hope that the advice, case studies and exercises in this book have provided you with the opportunity to unpack how your early experiences growing up influenced you and to explore how these may have informed your choices and shaped your beliefs, attitudes and identity.

By becoming clearer and more aware of your attachment style, hopefully you have seen how certain behaviours may show up and play out in your relationship. Being aware of how you behave is liberating because it gives you the opportunity to change negative patterns of thinking and behaving for more positive and constructive ones.

With a step-by-step approach to developing honest communication, intimacy, openness, trust and a willingness to work together and to be each other's greatest support during the happy and the tough times, you can ensure that your relationship is loving, strong, rewarding, fulfilling and that it lasts.

For the Future

By continuing to nurture and cherish your relationship, you will be able to give each other the joyful and healthy relationship model that will nourish you both. And, if you have children, then modelling for them how to build positive and meaningful relationships for themselves will be your relationship legacy.

References

1. Honeycutt, James M., and Bryan, Suzette P., *Scripts and Communication for Relationships* (Peter Lang Publishing Inc., 2010), 86
2. Fisher, Helen, *Why We Love: The Nature and Chemistry of Romantic Love* (Henry Holt, 2004) and Fisher, Helen, 'An fMRI study of a neural mechanism for mate choice', *The Journal of Comparative Neurology*, 493 (2005), 58–62
3. Mehrabian, A., and Ferris, S.R., 'Inference of Attitudes from Non-verbal Communication in Two Channels', *Journal of Consulting Psychology*, 31, 3 (1967) 48–258
4. Goleman, Daniel, *Emotional Intelligence* (Bloomsbury, 1996)
5. Figures based on 108 participants involved in gardening projects, walking groups, conservation work, running and cycling groups. 'Ecotherapy: The green agenda for mental health' (Mind week report, May 2007)
6. www.nhs.uk/conditions/postnataldepression
7. Holmes, Thomas, and Rahe, Richard, 'Social readjustment rating scale', *Journal of Psychosomatic Research*, 2 (1967), 214
8. Grant, H., 'The State of the Nation Report – Fractured Families' (2006). Available: http://www.scie-socialcareonline. org.uk/profile.asp?guid=6ECB23F0-7606-4987-A689-DCA762995094
9. Macallan, Dr Helen, 'Report on Infertility. Springfield Hospital in Tooting', *Daily Telegraph* (16 May 2003)
10. www.askforEDhelp.com
11. Miller, D., 'The "Sandwich" Generation: Adult Children of the Aging', *Social Work*, 26 (1981) 419–23
12. Cable, Dr Noriko (lead researcher), 'Friends are equally important to men and women, but family matters more for men's well-being', *Journal of Epidemiology & Community Health*, 67 (2013), 166–71

Further Reading

After the Affair: How to Build Trust and Love Again (Relate) by Julia Cole (Vermilion, 2010)

Before You Say 'I Do' (Relate) by Elizabeth Martyn (Vermilion, 2003)

Permanent Partners: Building Gay and Lesbian Relationships that Last by Betty Berzon, Ph.D. (Plume, 1990)

The Relate Guide to Finding Love by Barbara Bloomfield (Vermilion, 2009)

Relate Guide to Step-Families: Living Successfully with Other People's Children by Suzie Hayman (Vermilion, 2001)

Further Help

Relate
Relate is the UK's largest provider of relationship support, with over 70 years' experience in the field. Its services can be accessed face-to-face at a national network of Relate Centres and online or on the phone. Services range from: face-to-face counselling for couples, individuals and couples; sex therapy; counselling for children and young people; relationship skills courses and workshops; and family mediation.
www.relate.org.uk
0300 100 1234

British Association for Counselling & Psychotherapy
For information about how counselling can benefit you or those close to you, and how to find a private therapist who is relevant for your needs.
www.itsgoodtotalk.org.uk

The British Psychological Society
The British Psychological Society is the representative body for psychology and psychologists in the UK, and you can use their website to find a chartered psychologist.
www.bps.org.uk

Mind
Mind provides support and advice to anyone experiencing a mental-health problem. They also push for a better deal and respect for all people with mental-health problems. They provide direct support to almost 250,000 people each year.
www.mind.org.uk
Infoline: 0300 123 3393

Samaritans

The Samaritans offer a 24-hour helpline for people to talk about anything that is concerning them. You can talk to the Samaritans any time you like about whatever's getting to you – in your own way and off the record.
www.samaritans.org
UK: 08457 90 90 90, ROI: 1850 60 90 90

Pink Therapy

Pink Therapy is the UK's largest independent therapy organisation working with gender and sexual diversity clients.
www.pinktherapy.com

FFLAG

Friends and Family of Lesbians and Gays (FFLAG) offers support to local parents' groups and contacts in their efforts to help parents and families understand, accept and support their lesbian, gay and bisexual relatives with love and pride.
www.fflag.org.uk
0845 652 0311

Pace

A charity promoting mental health and emotional well-being for the lesbian, gay, bisexual and transgender community.
www.pacehealth.org.uk
020 7700 1323

National Childbirth Trust

National Childbirth Trust (NCT) provides support to parents, giving accurate, impartial information so that they can decide what's best for their family, and introducing them to a network of local parents to gain practical and emotional support.
www.nct.org.uk
Helpline: 0300 330 0700

Family Lives
Family Lives (previously called Parentline Plus) is a national
charity providing help and support in all aspects of family life.
You can chat with a trained support worker or share your
story on their forums.
www.familylives.org.uk
0808 800 2222

Cry-sis
Cry-sis offers support for families with excessively crying,
sleepless and demanding babies.
www.cry-sis.org.uk
Helpline: 08451 228 669 (9am–10pm)

National Family Mediation
National Family Mediation (NFM) mediators help clients to
reach joint decisions about the issues associated with their
separation – children, finance and property. Several NFM
services also provide specialist services for children.
www.nfm.org.uk
0300 4000 636

Age UK
Age UK (Age Concern and Help the Aged, now joined forces)
aim to improve later life for everyone through their information
and advice, services, campaigns, products, training and research.
www.ageuk.org.uk
0800 169 6565

Alzheimer's Society
Alzheimer's Society works to improve the quality of life of
people affected by dementia. Many of their 20,000 members
have personal experience of dementia, as carers, health
professionals or people with dementia themselves.
www.alzheimers.org.uk
Helpline: 0300 222 11 22

Macmillan Cancer Support

If you've been diagnosed with cancer, or a loved one has, Macmillan will support you every step of the way. They provide practical, medical and financial support and push for better cancer care.

www.macmillan.org.uk

0808 808 00 00

Cruse Bereavement Care

Cruse is committed to breaking the stigma around grief and ensuring that everyone, no matter how old or young, can access the highest-quality support following a bereavement. They have a telephone helpline and information on the website, and their trained volunteers provide face-to-face support and practical advice.

www.crusebereavementcare.org.uk

Daytime Helpline: 0844 477 9400

RD4U

RD4U is a website designed for young people by young people. It is part of Cruse Bereavement Care's Youth Involvement Project and is there to support young people after the death of someone close.

www.rd4u.org.uk

0808 808 1677

Acknowledgements

I want to express my deepest gratitude and heartfelt thanks to all those who made my book idea become a reality:

To Louise Francis at Vermilion, who believed in the idea, had faith in me and supported the project every step of the way. To Cath Allen at Relate, who encouraged me with enthusiasm, advice and bags of energy. To Barbara Broomfield at Relate, who spared the time to talk with me and share her knowledge and wisdom.

A big thank you to all the clients who I have counselled over the years, whose experiences, honesty and courage to share inspired this book.

To my husband Roy, for his constant love, positive encouragement and joy (and the many laughs we share daily). And my wonderful daughter, Anoushka, whose energy, passion for life and sense of fun is a joy to behold every single day.

Index